Questions That Every Writer Must Answer

—Where do good ideas come from?
—Should sentences and paragraphs be long or short?
—When should rules of grammar be obeyed, and when should they be stretched?
—Why does one piece of writing succeed, and another fail?
—How can you look at your own work and judge it fairly?

Whether you are a student writing a paper, a copywriter writing an ad, a business person writing a letter, a reporter writing a news story, an author writing a short story, novel, or nonfiction book, you will find all the ways to write it better in

100 WAYS TO IMPROVE YOUR WRITING

GARY PROVOST is a teacher of writing, as well as the author of over 1,000 stories and articles and ten fiction and non-fiction books, including FATAL DOSAGE and THE FREELANCE WRITER'S HANDBOOK, available in a Mentor edition.

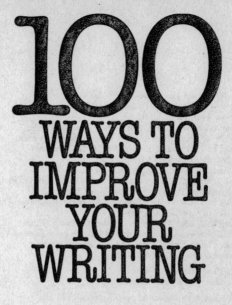

100
WAYS TO
IMPROVE
YOUR
WRITING

GARY PROVOST

A MENTOR BOOK

MENTOR
Published by New American Library, a division of
Penguin Group (USA) Inc., 375 Hudson Street,
New York, New York 10014, USA
Penguin Group (Canada), 90 Eglinton Avenue East, Suite 700, Toronto,
Ontario M4P 2Y3, Canada (a division of Pearson Penguin Canada Inc.)
Penguin Books Ltd., 80 Strand, London WC2R 0RL, England
Penguin Ireland, 25 St. Stephen's Green, Dublin 2,
Ireland (a division of Penguin Books Ltd.)
Penguin Group (Australia), 250 Camberwell Road, Camberwell, Victoria 3124,
Australia (a division of Pearson Australia Group Pty. Ltd.)
Penguin Books India Pvt. Ltd., 11 Community Centre, Panchsheel Park,
New Delhi - 110 017, India
Penguin Group (NZ), cnr Airborne and Rosedale Roads, Albany,
Auckland 1310, New Zealand (a division of Pearson New Zealand Ltd.)
Penguin Books (South Africa) (Pty.) Ltd., 24 Sturdee Avenue,
Rosebank, Johannesburg 2196, South Africa

Penguin Books Ltd., Registered Offices:
80 Strand, London WC2R 0RL, England

Published by Mentor, an imprint of New American Library,
a division of Penguin Group (USA) Inc.

First Printing, October 1985
30 29 28 27 26 25 24 23 22

Copyright © Gary Provost, 1972
All rights reserved

Ⓜ REGISTERED TRADEMARK—MARCA REGISTRADA

The Library of Congress Cataloging Card Number: 85-61266

Printed in the United States of America

Acknowledgments

Some of the material in this book appeared in different form in *Writer's Digest* magazine. I want to thank Bill Brohaugh, Rose Adkins, and Tom Clark at *Writer's Digest* for their work on the original articles.

At New American Library I want to thank Channah Taub, Andrea Stein, and Helen Eisenbach, each of whom watched over the book at some point.

And special thanks to Claudia Reilly, who edited the book at New American Library, and to Jon Matson.

Also I want to gratefully acknowledge permission to reprint the following material:

Excerpt from *Dandelion Wine* by Ray Bradbury. Copyright © 1975, Ray Bradbury. Reprinted with the permission of Doubleday and Co.

Excerpt from *Psychology Today,* Copyright © 1983.

Excerpt from *The Great Gatsby* by F. Scott Fitzgerald. Copyright © 1926 Charles Scribner's Sons; copyright renewed 1953 Frances Scott Fitzgerald Lanahan. Reprinted with the permission of Charles Scribner's Sons.

Excerpt from *The Sun Also Rises* by Ernest Hemingway. Copyright © 1926 Charles Scribner's Sons; copyright renewed 1954 Ernest Hemingway. Reprinted with the permission of Charles Scribner's Sons.

Excerpt from the *Boston Globe* by John Bierman. Copyright © 1983, John Bierman. Reprinted with the permission of John Bierman.

Excerpt from "Kelly's Gift" by James Ricci, *Reader's Digest,* June 1983.

Excerpt from *No Time For Sergeants* by Mac Hyman. Copyright © 1954 by Mac Hyman. Reprinted with the permission of Random House, Inc.

Dedication

As a free-lance writer I live and die by the mailbox. During the past twenty years I have sent and received more than forty thousand pieces of mail that had some part of my heart attached to them. And during that time there haven't been more than one or two mishaps concerning the handling of my mail. Though I have laughed at post-office jokes and have made a few myself, the fact is that the United States Postal Service has the highest success record of any business I have ever dealt with. For that reason this book is dedicated to the men and women of the post office at South Lancaster, Massachusetts 01561, and to postal workers everywhere.

Contents

CONTENTS

CONTENTS

CONTENTS

CONTENTS

Introduction

This book will teach you how to write better ransom notes.

It will also teach you how to write better love letters, short stories, magazine articles, letters to the editor, business proposals, sermons, poems, novels, parole requests, church newsletters, songs, memos, essays, term papers, theses, graffiti, death threats, advertisements, and shopping lists.

If your writing does not improve after you read this book, you have not failed. I have. It is the writer's job, not the reader's, to see that writing accomplishes whatever goal the writer has set for it.

One bit of advice I will give you in this book is "Make yourself likable." Readers who like you are more inclined to trust you, to laugh at your jokes, cry over your anguish, sign the petition, buy the product, put the check in the mail, or do whatever else it is you are trying to get them to do through your writing.

I want you to like me so that you will follow my

advice—and recommend my book to your friends. And that's important for you to know because it means I am on your side. I'm not here to tell you that you're writing wrong. I'm here to show you how to write right.

CHAPTER ONE

Nine Ways to Improve Your Writing When You're Not Writing

1. Get Some Reference Books

2. Expand Your Vocabulary

3. Improve Your Spelling

4. Read

5. Take a Class

6. Eavesdrop

7. Research

8. Write in Your Head

9. Choose a Time and Place

1. Get Some Reference Books

It would be a shame to bring an entire writing project to a halt just because you didn't know how to spell *gyroscope* or *schnapps*. So get a dictionary and keep it in the room where you write, no more than an arm's length away. In fact, get two. Get a hard cover for its comprehensiveness and a paperback for convenience.

Also, get an encyclopedia. If you can't afford a big set, get a single volume encyclopedia.

And get a thesaurus. *Thesaurus* means "treasury"; the thesaurus you buy will be a treasury of synonyms, words that are close in meaning to the one you want. It is a book that will lead you to that perfect word you know is loitering on the outskirts of your brain.

Roget's Thesaurus is arranged in two sections. The first section contains hundreds of clusters of related words and phrases. The second section is an index listing all the words in the first section alphabetically and telling you where they appear in that section.

Let's say, for example, that in a letter you want to

assure the owner of the company you work for that you will most certainly try to recover the four billion dollars you lost on the papier-mâché deal, but *recover* isn't quite the word you want to use, and you're not sure what is. So you whip out your pocket edition of *Roget's Thesaurus*, turn to the index, and look up *recover*. There you'll find the numbers 660, 775, and 790. You turn to cluster 660 and you find *recover* along with its cousins *rally, revive, pull through, reappear,* and others. If you don't like anything you find there, you turn to the other numbers, and the thesaurus will lead you to *redeem, get back, salvage,* and so on.

You can find thesauruses in paperback and hard cover, and *Roget's* is not the only one. I do not recommend the ones that are arranged solely in dictionary form. They are easier to use but only about twelve percent as useful.

After you have acquired a dictionary, an encyclopedia, and a thesaurus, you can acquire other reference books as time, taste, and money allow. Their importance depends largely on what sort of writing you do and how much.

Here are a few reference books you might find useful.

Finding Facts Fast by Alden Todd (Ten Speed Press) is a good reference book for any writer who has to do research.

The *Statistical Abstract of the United States* will tell you how many tomatoes were grown in New Jersey last year and a good many other things you might not find anywhere else. You can order it from the U.S. Government Printing Office, Washington, D.C. 20402.

The Book of Lists by David Wallechinsky, Irving Wallace, and Amy Wallace (Bantam) is fun to read and rich with useful information.

The Help Book by J. L. Barkas (Scribner's) will tell you who provides what services and where you can get more information.

The King's English by H. W. Fowler and F. G. Fowler (Oxford University Press) is an excellent grammar text.

Words into Type (Prentice-Hall) will guide you through every aspect of manuscript preparation, from matters of usage and grammar to matters of editing and proofreading.

2. Expand Your Vocabulary

Everybody has heard tips for improving vocabulary. Learn a new word in the morning and use it three times before sunset and it's yours, etc. There are many books that will help you stretch your vocabulary. The best known one is *Thirty Days to a More Powerful Vocabulary* by Wilfred Funk and Norman Lewis (Funk and Wagnalls). Read that book or one like it.

But the most important vocabulary for the writer is not the one that will take in *uxorious* tomorrow and *soubrette* the next day. It's the one he or she already has. For the writer of average intelligence and education, learning new words is much less important than learning to use easily the words he or she already knows.

Think for a minute. How many synonyms can you come up with for the noun *plan*?

There are *program, itinerary, scheme, design, agenda, outline,* and *blueprint.* If you concentrated for a minute, you might have come up with ten words that you already knew. But how many of them would have come easily to mind while you were writing a letter to the boss about your potentially lucrative new . . . uh . . . plan?

The only way to make your vocabulary more accessible is to use it. If you want all those short but interesting words waiting at the front of your brain when you need them, you must move them to the front of your brain before you need them.

Stop to think about other word possibilities when you write, and eventually they will come so quickly that you won't have to stop.

Pause before you speak. Then insert some of those good but neglected words.

And when you drive home from work at night, pick out an object along the road and see how many synonyms you can think of before you pass it. There's a house over there. But it's also a dwelling, an abode, a building, a bungalow, perhaps, or maybe a cottage. It's a home for somebody, it's headquarters for a family, and it's a shelter and a structure, too.

3. Improve Your Spelling

There aren't many firm rules that apply to the spelling of English words. Mostly, good spelling is a matter of forming the right mental associations and developing an eye for words that look a little weird.

In the dictionary, look up any word that you're not sure of. If you have been misspelling it, write it correctly ten times. Invent a visual image for the correct spelling. For example: The Sahara *desert* only has one *s*, like Sahara, but the *dessert* after a meal has a second *s*, like a second helping.

How will better spelling improve your writing? Well, for one thing, you won't write *desert* when you mean *dessert*. More important, it will improve your writing by reducing the number of times you annoy the reader. A few misspelled words will jar the reader's concentration, and a lot of misspelled words will wreck your credibility. Right or wrong, the reader will perceive you as . . . well, stupid, to put it bluntly. If you don't have the respect of the reader, your writing will not work.

Fifty of the Most Commonly Misspelled Words:

acceptable	fascinate	orchestra
apology	grateful	potatoes
appetite	hygiene	professor
architect	imaginable	pseudonym
assassinate	immediately	quarrelsome
autumn	irrelevant	religious
calendar	jewelry	reservoir
changeable	judgment	rhythmic
conscious	lovable	scissors
correspondence	miscellaneous	syllable
criticism	mischievous	tragedy
deceive	mortgage	umbrella
discernible	necessarily	vanilla
embarrass	occasionally	vengeance
eminent	occurrence	weird

existence   omission   wholesome
youthful
zealot

4. Read

If you are an a architect, you should certainly read architectural literature. If you are in computers, you must keep up with what's being written about bits and bytes, demodulation and interlaced fields. Reading the books and trade magazines of your particular field will not only keep you informed, it will show you how experienced writers are turning the jargon and the complexities of your vocation into readable prose.

But no matter what your field of expertise, you should also read books, magazines, and newspapers designed for the general reader.

Though the daily paper contains much that is swill, it also contains some good writing. From it you can learn to write leanly, you can learn to get to the point, and you can learn to compress several facts into a single clear sentence.

If you read paperback detective novels and romances, you will discover how writers create curiosity, and build tension. You will also learn how to construct an event, a person, or a place with just a few well-chosen words.

Read major novels. You will see how words can be used to communicate subtleties and stir emotions, how words can be arranged one way to make you worry, another to make you laugh.

Read magazine articles and you will see how quotes are pared down from lengthy interviews until they contain nothing but the words that matter. Notice how opinions are supported by facts. Watch to see how the writer makes his points by calling on outside help such as scientific reports, quotes from books, surveys, etc.

Read. And listen to what you read. Listen for the sound of the language, the music. Note the punctuation, the spelling, the logical progression of information. And find the things that fail, also. Listen to how two similiar sounds close together can cause a disturbing noise in your head. Hear how the use of the wrong word wakes you from your reading spell. Be a critical reader, and look upon all that you read as a lesson in good writing.

5. Take a Class

If you don't believe that good writing can be taught, you shouldn't be reading this book. If you do believe good writing can be taught, you could benefit from a class.

You don't have to sign up for a three-credit course at the local university. You can find a creative writing or English composition course in most adult education and extension programs.

There are specific courses designed for particular types of writers. For example, there are business writing courses that thoroughly cover the formal English required in business correspondence. A course in nonfiction writing will provide you with some research techniques that you wouldn't get elsewhere. And a course in writing for television would be invaluable if that's your interest, as there are many rules of form a scriptwriter must follow.

Generally, a writing course is as good or as bad as the teacher. Good teachers and bad teachers are found at all levels, so ask around.

Whether it's a course at the local high school or a course at Harvard, in my opinion you should steer clear of any teacher who speaks with a British accent but has never been to England and any teacher who insists you must read *Moby Dick* before writing your first paper. Point yourself toward the eager, unpretentious teacher who is actually publishing stories, articles, and books.

"But why," you ask, "should I take a writing class at all after reading a wonderful book like this?"

Good question. Three answers.

1. With a teacher and other students reading your work, you will be better able to learn what your particular faults and virtues are.

2. Knowing that the class or teacher is going to read your work, you will work harder at making your writing good.

3. Your own writing mistakes are often invisible to you, but they will become obvious when you see them in the work of fellow students.

6. Eavesdrop

Be nosy. Listen to conversations on the bus, in the elevator. Screen out the words sometimes and listen only to the music. Tune in to teenagers' conversations, and you'll pick up the latest slang. Pretend to be reading on the park bench, and you'll hear how words are used to convey more than they mean. Find out what people are talking about, what they care about. All of this will help you to communicate more effectively through your writing.

This passage from my book *The Dorchester Gas Tank* is based on a conversation I overheard at a diner in Burlington, Vermont.

> *"My neighbor's daughter has just got back from Sweden,"* Bernice *says. Her words are slightly muffled because she has stopped in her conversation with Dora to slice open a roll of Italian bread and stuff it with provolone cheese, several thick slices of baloney and enough tomatoes, onions, etc. to sink a ship. Now she chomps on it as if food will soon be obsolete.*
>
> *"I didn't know they went to Europe,"* Bernice's *sister says.*
>
> *"Well it's not really Europe. It's in Scandinavia. It's a Danish country."*
>
> *"Oh yes,"* Dora *says,* *"the Danish country is very nice, but those people don't like to talk to outsiders."*
>
> *"Well, it's a sub-language they speak,"* Bernice *says.* *"It's like German, not fully developed."*
>
> *"Very guttural,"* Dora *says.*
>
> *"My neighbor's daughter says some of them are*

*really awful. She went to a cathedral and one of them
had stolen a crown from a statue of the Blessed Mother.''*
''From the Blessed Mother? That's disgraceful.''

7. Research

Do your fingers sometimes freeze over the typewriter
keyboard? Does the paper seem to stare back at you with
an accusing eye? The problem could be that you haven't
gathered enough information. You haven't gotten the facts.

Almost everything you will ever write must be built on a
foundation of factual information. That includes opinion
pieces and most certainly includes stories, plays, and novels.

Before you write, track down the bits of information
you are going to need. Get the prices you must quote, the
names of people you will mention. Find out when it's
going to happen, where it will be, who's going to be
speaking, and whether or not dogs are allowed. You cannot write securely on any subject unless you have gathered
far more information than you will use.

Here are four ways to get facts.

1. Look it up. If the facts are not in the books on your
shelf, try the company library or the public library. Through
the library system, you have access to just about every
piece of information in the world, though in some cases
the information might have been printed only in Swahili.

2. Ask somebody. Who has the information you need?
Is it the chairperson of the canvassing committee? Is it the
president of the company? Is it the president's secretary?

Ask yourself, "Who would know?" Then go directly to the most logical and best-informed people. And if anybody begins an answer with "Well, gee, Harry, I think maybe that now that you ask, let me see . . ." ask somebody else.

3. Observe it. Sometimes the best way to acquire facts is to conduct an experiment. Do you need to know how many miles it is from the center of town to the church? Drive from downtown to the church and check your mileage. Will people in wheelchairs be able to attend the dinner at the Old Timer's Café? Go to the Old Timer's, have a drink. And while you are there, look for ramps, measure the doorways, check the rest rooms.

Of course, there's not always time for this sort of thing. In an emergency, ask somebody. Like a waitress at the Old Timer's, or the minister who's got to drive downtown to put the collection in the bank.

4. Speak to the reference librarian. Most libraries offer a reference service. Use it. When you need information and you don't know where to find it, ask the librarian. He or she will find it, or direct you to the source. Many libraries will handle reference questions over the phone, and that can spare you a good deal of frustration when your writing comes to a standstill because you don't know where George Gershwin was born. Keep the library's phone number handy. But remember that librarians are the servants of ignorance, not of laziness. Call the librarian if you need to know the biggest crops in Bolivia, but don't call to ask how Bolivia is spelled.

8. Write in Your Head

When I was a reporter for a local newspaper, I used to leave a school committee or selectmen's meeting around eleven P.M. in Hudson and drive eight miles to the newspaper office in Marlboro, where I would write my stories for the next day's edition.

Often I arrived after other reporters. But almost invariably I would write my stories, hand them in, and drive home before the others. I was able to do this, not because I am a faster typist, but because I started writing before I got to the office. I wrote the first draft in my head during the drive to Marlboro. In my mind I planned the lead, decided what information I could ignore, and organized my material. By the time I reached the office, I knew what I wanted to write, and when I sat down at the typewriter, it was like pushing the "play" button on a tape recorder. Everything I had recorded in my brain came out.

So if you have a writing job, write in your head. Clear up the inconsistencies while you're brushing your teeth. Get your thoughts organized while you're driving to work. Think of a slant during lunch. And most important, come up with a beginning, a lead, so that you won't end up staring at your typewriter as if it had just arrived from another galaxy. If you have spent time writing in your head, you'll have a head start. The writing will come easier, and you'll finish sooner.

9. Choose a Time and Place

For most writers the hardest part of any writing project is getting started. I often begin by staring at the typewriter as if it is some vile substance that has been spilled on my desk. Then, no matter how alert I was when I arrived at the typewriter, I become almost terminally drowsy. My eyes droop. My shoulders sag. Finally, I begin to think, "Well, maybe I should take a little nap first, then I'll be well rested for writing." Usually my puritan conscience cancels that plan. So I take on the expression of a man who has just been strapped into a dentist's chair and begin to write. As soon as I have words on paper, agony departs. I love writing. It's getting started that I abhor.

I tell you this so that you won't feel alone. You probably go through similar hell before you write. Almost everybody does. The way to eliminate most of these traumas is to write in large blocks of time rather than try to write for ten minutes here and ten minutes there. Look at your schedule. When will you be left undisturbed for an hour or two? Can you lock the door? Unplug the phone? You will get more writing done in an undisturbed hour than you would in a dozen ten-minute spurts.

It is also important to find a quiet place to write. Few people can write their best when the phone is ringing and the kids are clamoring for whatever it is that makes kids clamor. A den in a noisy house would probably produce less writing than the back seat of a car in a quiet garage. So find someplace quiet. Is there a day when everybody else is out of the house? Does a friend have a cottage? Does your company have an empty office?

If you can't find a quiet place to write, use earplugs.

CHAPTER TWO

Nine Ways to Overcome Writer's Block

1. Copy Something

2. Keep a Journal

3. Talk About What You're Writing

4. Touch Your Toes

5. Do Writing Exercises

6. Organize Your Material

7. Make a List

8. Picture a Reader

9. Ask Yourself Why You Are Writing

1. Copy Something

Yes, copy. From time to time take a few paragraphs from something that you enjoyed reading and sit down at the typewriter or with a notebook and copy them word for word. You will find yourself suddenly aware of the choices the writer made. You will look at the work from the writer's point of view. In time you will feel like an insider, and you will say, "I know why he chose this word; I know why he made two short sentences here instead of one long one." You will become more intimate with the writer's words and with words in general, and your own writing will be better for it.

If you don't have a favorite passage to copy, use this one from *The Great Gatsby* (Scribner's) by F. Scott Fitzgerald. It's a favorite of mine.

His heart beat faster and faster as Daisy's white face came up to his own. He knew that when he kissed this girl, and forever wed his unutterable visions to her perishable breath, his mind would never romp again like the mind of God. So he waited, listening for a moment longer to the tuning fork that had been struck upon a star. Then he kissed her. At his lips' touch she blossomed for him like a flower and the incarnation was complete.

Through all he said, even through his appalling sentimentality, I was reminded of something—an elusive rhythm, a fragment of lost words, that I had heard somewhere a long time ago. For a moment a phrase tried to take shape in my mouth and my lips parted like a dumb man's, as though there was more struggling upon them than a wisp of startled air. But they made no sound, and what I had almost remembered was uncommunicable forever.

2. Keep a Journal

There is no one right way to keep a journal. But if you have some sort of notebook or diary that you return to often with your written thoughts, opinions, observations, and various bits of wit, you will have a place in which to exercise your writing muscles.

You will learn to describe succinctly and clearly the events of your daily life. You will learn to pluck from each event just the details needed to create a sense of the whole. If you keep a journal, you will grow as a writer, and you will find that sooner or later, no matter what you have to write professionally, your personal experiences will play a part.

Keep in mind, however, that a journal can be far more than just a diary. You can take notes from a conversation. You can take notes while you're reading, or eating at a restaurant. You can even take notes while you're watching television. I know of one woman who took notes while watching the National Cheerleading Competition on TV. She learned all the terms, and with the information she gathered, she was able to make a story about a cheerleader convincing.

3. Talk About What You're Writing

When you're looking for a job, you tell as many people as you can. There's always the chance that one of your friends knows about a suitable job opening, or that someone knows a guy who knows a guy, etc. Same thing when you want to buy a house. You tell people what size house you're looking for, how much you can spend, and what kind of neighbors you can't stand. You do this because maybe somebody has heard about a house you'd want to buy. In effect, by telling people what you need, you plug into a huge computer loaded with all the relevant information your friends have accumulated.

When you have a story to write, plug into that computer. Talk about your story. Tell people your subject and your particular slant. Chances are your friend Karen read a book last week that had a chapter on your subject, your cousin Louie might send you an appropriate newspaper clipping, somebody else might remember a fitting quote from George Bernard Shaw, and your brother James might remember something significant that he heard when he was in prison.

4. Touch Your Toes

Do a little warm-up exercise before you write. If your toes are too far away to touch, then stretch your arms or dance or jump up and down. Whatever. James Michener actually goes into physical training like a boxer before he begins a book, so the least you can do is take a few deep breaths, put your pulse rate into second gear, and deliver a supply of oxygen to the brain. All of this will improve the clarity of your thinking and the quality of your energy.

Also, do not continue to write after you become fatigued. A tired writer at the typewriter is as dangerous as a tired driver behind the steering wheel. If your eyes begin to droop and your head wobbles, stand up and do some more exercise. That should rejuvenate you. If it doesn't, take a nap.

5. Do Writing Exercises

Just as you need to get your body warmed up to run, you need a little writing exercise before starting a writing project.

A writing exercise can be almost anything that turns thoughts into words. Make a list of ten rhyming words. Describe the inside of a Ping-Pong ball. But whatever you do, do it in a noncritical way. Turn off the editor in your head. The exercise is not supposed to be polished prose any more than a warm-up run is supposed to set a world record.

6. Organize Your Material

Certainly there is such a thing as being overorganized. Some writers organize their material so thoroughly that everything they write comes out looking like a hardware catalog. Your outline, whatever its form, should contain enough slack for creativity and space for new thoughts on your subject.

But you should organize the material. Organizing will help lock in the logic of what you say, and it will speed the writing process. Organizing will help to create an overall unity in your story as well as several interior unities.

There is no one right way to organize material for a story. Organization depends on the nature of the work and, more importantly, on what works for you. So I cannot offer you the best way to organize material. But I will give you a few tips:

• Create a list of questions about your subject before you begin research, and keep related questions together.

Go to many different sources for answers—even go to many sources for answers to a single question. Several answers to the same question are compelling when they are similar and fascinating when they are not.

• Gather much more material than you will use. Just as high water pressure makes more water flow faster, the greater weight of material you have gathered will make the words flow faster.

• As you create written material, whether you are photocopying at the library, transcribing taped interviews, or simply scribbling notes, write on one side of the paper only. That way you can slice up your material with a pair of scissors and rearrange it any way you want.

7. Make a List

Some writers will not write a magazine article until they have constructed an outline that is longer than the article they intend to write. Other writers begin with no outline at all, though they probably have a vague outline in mind.

How long or detailed your outline is depends on the scope of what you have to write and how secure you are with the material. But an outline is just a list of elements you want to put into your writing, and for any story or article you should make some sort of list, even if it's just three words scribbled on a scrap of paper. Write some key words for the issues you want to cover, the facts you want to point to, the questions you want to pose. Glance at the list as you work. This will help you decide what to write next.

If, for example, you want to write a letter to your lawyer describing the skullduggery your husband has been up to since the divorce agreement was signed, you might scribble a list that looks like this:

1. *Cheated me on the car payments.*
2. *Sends support checks late.*
3. *Tells the kids lies.*

Even if you are writing something short, such as a press release, it's a good idea to make a list of essential elements. Making a checklist: "Time. Date. Place. Price." Newspaper offices are always getting press releases that don't mention what time the pancake breakfast at the Boys' Club begins.

8. Picture a Reader

Do you know who your reader is? Is your story going to be read by a professor who knows everything but has very little time? Or is the reader a layperson with no knowledge of your specialty? A little girl, perhaps? An immigrant?

Before you write, figure out whom you are trying to reach. Who is the reader and what does he or she know?

To write is not necessarily to communicate. Communication occurs in the mind of the reader, and if that reader is not familiar with your terms and your concepts, you might as well write them in Latvian. The computer terms that are impressive in a letter to your software engineer will be gobbledygook in a sales brochure aimed at people who have never used computers.

Remember that when you write, the language you have to work with is not your entire vocabulary, but only that portion of it that you share with the reader. Just because you speak Portuguese doesn't mean you should pepper your story with Portuguese phrases. This reminder goes not just for words but for historical allusions and the like. When you write, don't think about how smart you are; think about how smart your reader is. To do that you must visualize him or her. Imagine your reader in the room with you. What is his education? What are his attitudes? How important is this particular story to him? Write as if you were in conversation with your readers. Listen to the dialogue that would occur. Are your readers going to stop you and say, "Wait a minute, wait a minute, what's a *grumdocle*?" If they are, then don't use *grumdocle*, or explain it when you do.

9. Ask Yourself Why You Are Writing

Do not write until you know why you are writing. What are your goals? Are you trying to make readers laugh? Are you trying to persuade them to buy a product? Are you trying to advise them? Are you trying to inform them so that they can make a decision?

If you cannot answer the question "Why am I writing

this?'' then you cannot wisely choose words, provide facts, include or exclude humor. You must know what job you want done before you can pick the tools to do it. And if you cannot state clearly at least one reason for writing your story, article, or paper . . . don't write it.

CHAPTER THREE

Five Ways to Write a Strong Beginning

1. Find a Slant

2. Write a Strong Lead

3. Don't Make Promises You Can't Keep

4. Set a Tone and Maintain It

5. Begin at the Beginning

1. Find a Slant

Do not try to write everything about your subject. All subjects are inexhaustible. If you try to write on every aspect of your subject, you will ramble. You will get lost in the writing, your wastebasket will overflow, and you will become a crazy person. Tie yourself to a specific idea about your subject, some aspect that is manageable. That aspect is called the slant. Here are some examples.

Unslanted Idea	Slanted Idea
Stained Glass Windows	The History of Stained Glass Windows
	How to Photograph Stained Glass Windows
	Stained Glass Windows on Essex Street: Beauty in the City
Absenteeism	The Cost of Absenteeism in This Corporation

The Vietnam War	*How Much Did Vietnam Cost Us?*
	What We Learned From Vietnam
	The Vietnam War; Is It Really Over?

2. Write a Strong Lead

There is no precise definition of the lead. It can be the first sentence, the first paragraph, even the first several paragraphs of your article or story. The lead is whatever it takes to lead your readers so deeply into your story or article that they will not turn back unless you stray from the path you have put them on.

Here are two leads that I have used recently.

On a clear day in Salem you can stand in front of the Peabody Museum and stare down Essex Sreet all the way to the Hawthorne Boulevard. And, if you're in luck, you might see something black coming around the corner, something black and bewildering, floating, like a hole in the sky growing larger as it comes toward you. For an instant it is as disturbing as a rustle in the night. Don't be concerned. It is only Laurie Cabot.

John E. Rock kills people for their own good.
"It's all hypothetical, of course," he says, waving a

hand at his Basic Four Computer in the Framingham office of Rock Insurance.

Though the term "lead" is usually associated with non-fiction, the lead in fiction is just as important. Here is how Gail Levine-Freidus began her novel for children *Popcorn* (Bradbury Press).

You know how sometimes you suddenly get the feeling that someone is watching every move you make? The feeling sort of sneaks up on you and gives you the creeps, whatever they are. Well that's exactly how I felt in Mr. Pettigrew's English class just as I was starting to work on the last section of our test.

A lead should be provocative. It should have energy, excitement, an implicit promise that something is going to happen or that some interesting information will be revealed. It should create curiosity, get the reader asking questions.

The character of a good lead depends largely on the nature and length of what you have written. A 500-word lead in an 800-word story is not a good lead, but it could be a great lead in a 3,000-word story.

Your lead should give readers something to care about before it gives them dry background information. "Something to care about" usually means one of two things. Either you give the readers information which affects them directly, or you give them a human being with whom they can identify.

Don't begin a story in the company newsletter like this:

On March 27 the Board of Directors met at the Holiday Inn in Podunk. All but two members were present. John Burdick of the Tymecomp Agency presented the results of his time and productivity study. Mr. Burdick has spent six months in the four plants surveying daily production, employee attendance records, and overhead costs. He has spoken to employees and personnel managers. He described the effectiveness of a variety of work schedules, and on his recommendation the board voted unanimously to put the company on a four-day workweek, effective June 1.

Employees would have to read the whole first paragraph before they found what the story had to do with them. Most employees would not have bothered.

The provocative information, the information that will hook the reader and compel him to keep reading, is at the end of the paragraph. It should be moved to the front, and the lead should be:

On June 1 the company will go on a four-day work week.

This next lead is from a story about a dangerous antitermite chemical. It was written by John Bierman and appeared in *The Boston Globe*. Instead of loading his lead with impersonal background material, Bierman brought his story immediately to life by giving the reader something to care about. Note the two important elements in Bierman's lead: he made it *visible*—he showed us something; and he made it *human*—he showed us what the problem means to some real people.

NEW YORK—Jeffrey Lever had his split level ranch house in East Islip, Long Island bulldozed to the ground with all its contents last week after it was discovered the house's interior had been sprayed with a potentially lethal chemical.

A lead like that will make your reader want to keep reading.

One common mistake you should be aware of is the writing of two or three leads in the same story. Often a writer creates a good lead and then repeats all the information in the second paragraph, and again in the third.

This also is from a story that appeared in *The Boston Globe*:

Terminally ill nuclear power plant projects never die quickly. They are killed slowly by public criticism, hostile regulators, persistent conservation, climbing construction costs and an appetite for cash that Wall Street refuses to meet.

Despite regulatory attacks, conservation, skyrocketing construction costs and threatened problems in raising cash, the nuclear plants rising on the beach at Seabrook, N.H. are far from dead.

The second paragraph of that article would have made the better lead. It contains all the information in the first paragraph plus a specific statement of interest to the reader. If the writer had inserted the phrase "problems which typically kill nuclear plants," the first paragraph could have been tossed in the wastebasket.

3. Don't Make Promises You Can't Keep

Science has found a cure for cancer.

Is that a good lead? It is if science has found a cure for cancer. But it's not a good lead if the writer goes on to write, "Of course, nothing is definite yet," and "Dr. Inman's theories have not been fully tested," and "The serum has never been tried on human beings." Then the lead becomes a trick, a dishonest way of getting the readers into the story, and they will feel cheated after reading the article.

A lead is not strong if it does not deliver on the promises it makes. Anybody can write a lead that will attract attention, but if the lead is not supported by what follows, it will do more harm than good.

4. Set a Tone and Maintain It

Almost every arena of activity conveys some message about the tone or mood in which it is to be experienced. You are not expected to laugh out loud at a hanging, but it's okay to laugh at a Woody Allen movie. You shouldn't scream when you find a great bargain at Macy's, but it's okay to scream at the carnival when the Tilt-a-Whirl spins you around. (Throwing up is also acceptable.) In life, mixed messages about tone, such as gag napkins at a wake, are disturbing. The same is true in reading.

In your opening paragraph you set a tone. Your choice of words, your arrangement of those words, and your choice of information all convey to the reader some message about the tone of the story. In some way the writer, you, makes an announcement such as "This is urgent," or "Let's be practical," or "Let's laugh at this."

The following passage becomes "wrong" when the writer creates a sudden and jarring shift in tone. He begins with a tone that is urgent, cruel, and efficient, but he switches to a tone that is poetic, leisurely, and analytical. Readers, believing they knew the writer's attitude toward the material, are suddenly not so sure!

Myron slammed the gate behind him and walked straight up to the cop on duty. "Now," he said, "I want that scum now." The cop moved quickly to block the door. But Myron was quicker. He rammed a fist into the cop's gut, and when the cop keeled forward, Myron sliced a karate chop into the back of his neck. The cop dropped with a thud. Myron yanked open the door to the cellblock. He ran down the corridor to cell 9. He pulled open his jacket and grabbed the pistol from his holster. "Arrivederci, scum!" he cried at Demetrius. There was a pitiful shriek, the blast of gunfire, then the panicky screaming of other prisoners who feared a massacre.

It was cool there in the cellblock, as cool as those distant mornings back in Trenton when Myron was a boy. The air here was light and refreshing, like a sparkling tonic brought in to douse the heat of the day. Even the cement walls around the cellblock had been painted a cool and soothing aqua, and on one end a mural of colorful birds enhanced the sense of calm. Myron was pleased with what he had done. For a moment he pretended that he was still sitting on the highest branch of that old cottonwood tree in Trenton, and he sipped slowly the heady air of success.

5. Begin at the Beginning

Many writers work their way into a paper, letter, or story as if they were feeling their way into a dark house. They use the first few pages, and sometimes considerably more, as a kind of writing warm-up. There's nothing wrong with writing three pages of junk before you get to information that matters, as long as those three pages are extinct before the final draft. In other words, don't include your warm-up exercises with the manuscript.

Study the beginning of your story carefully. You might discover that with the first 200 words you are "getting around to telling the story." Look at the first sentence. Is it substantive? Is it doing some work? Or is it merely background information *about* what you haven't quite begun yet?

Bad	Better
I'm writing this memo because Sam Moroni has fled the country, and I need to replace him quickly.	*Sam Moroni has fled the country, and I need to replace him quickly.*

Obviously, no one is going to stop reading a memo because of five unnecessary words, but many writers use three pages to say "I'm writing this because . . ."

Cross out every sentence until you come to one you cannot do without. That is your beginning.

CHAPTER FOUR

Nine Ways to Save Time and Energy

1. Use Pyramid Construction

2. Use Topic Sentences

3. Write Short Paragraphs

4. Use Transitional Phrases

5. Don't Explain When You Don't Have To

6. Use Bridge Words

7. Avoid Wordiness

8. Steal

9. Stop Writing When you Get to the End

1. Use Pyramid Construction

Writing in the pyramid style means getting to the point at the top, putting the "who, what, when, where, and why" in the first paragraph, and developing the supporting information under it.

Newspapers use pyramid style because they are in the business of getting facts to readers as quickly as possible and because of the way news stories must be edited. When a newspaper editor has a seven-inch story that he or she has to put into a six-inch hole in the newspaper, that editor doesn't run through the story with a pencil looking for useless adverbs or sentences that can be rewritten. He or she simply cuts an inch off the bottom. That is why each inch of a pyramid-style story should be less important than the inch that came before it.

You should use pyramid style for any short report and for any story that might be cut. And when you do, don't put anything in paragraph 12 that the reader must know in order to understand paragraph 7.

Without Pyramid Construction	With Pyramid Construction
The flames could still be seen at dawn, flickering lights at the bottom of the canyon. Ethyl Murdock stood by, chuckling. "That'll show them Detroit folks," she said.	*Mrs. Ethyl Murdock of Elgin, Illinois pushed her new Dodge van off a cliff yesterday afternoon after the truck broke down for the sixteenth time since she bought it just a week ago.*
Ethyl Murdock had just pushed her brand new Dodge van off a cliff when she spoke those words . . .	*At dawn today the flames from the van could still be seen flickering . . .*

2. Use Topic Sentences

A topic sentence in a paragraph is a sentence containing the thought that is developed throughout the rest of the paragraph. The topic sentence is commonly the first sentence in a paragraph.

Deciding what to put in a paragraph and what to leave out will be easier if you first write a topic sentence. For each paragraph ask, "What do I want to say here? What point do I want to make? What question do I want to present?" Answer with a single general sentence. That is your topic sentence. Chances are that the topic sentence will fall neatly into the paragraph it inspires. But even if you don't include the topic sentence in your paragraph, it will serve as a guide. When you rewrite your early drafts, ask how each sentence in a paragraph supports the topic sentence of the paragraph. If the answer is "It doesn't," then ask what other work the sentence is doing in the paragraph. If the answer is "None," get rid of the sentence.

Here are two paragraphs from magazine articles. The first paragraph begins with a topic sentence. The second paragraph ends with a topic sentence. But note that in each one all the sentences support or "prove" the statement made in the topic sentence.

Topic Sentence Begins Paragraph

Kelly's condition deteriorated further on Monday. Her pupils became dilated and unresponsive to light. An electroencephalogram done at 8:30 Tuesday morning detected no signs of brain activity. A second one done on Wednesday was similarly negative. That afternoon a neurosurgeon informed Kelly's parents that their child was, in fact, dead.

(from Reader's Digest, *June 1983)*

Topic Sentence Concludes Paragraph

Burke's experience is borne out by a growing body of research that overturns some of the widespread popular assumptions about moving. In a number of recent studies, spouses and children of peripatetic executives are shown to have survived the traumas of moving in far better shape than popular myth indicates, and the breadwinners themselves have emerged relatively unscathed. The upshot seems to be that frequent job related moves need not be bad for you.

(from Psychology Today, *June 1983)*

3. Write Short Paragraphs

Your writing will be faster, livelier, and clearer if you write short paragraphs. The reader will welcome the break and the white space. You will be less likely to get tied up in verbal knots. Your thoughts will be better organized and more succinctly expressed. You and the reader will find it easier to locate specific statements.

4. Use Transitional Phrases

A transition in writing is a word or group of words that moves the reader from one place to another. The "place" might be the location of a scene, a spot in time, or an area of discussion. The transition should be quick, smooth, quiet, reliable, and logical. And it should bring to itself a minimum of attention.

Transitions are important because they represent passage through a "danger zone" where you risk losing your reader. You use a transition to show the reader the connection between what he has just read and what he is about to read by implying the relationship between those two bodies of information. Here are some common transitional phrases:

Transitions of Time	Transitions of Place
The following week . . .	*On the other side of the mountain . . .*
In December of that year . . .	*In Black Eagle, Montana . . .*
By the time Renaldo arrived . . .	*Meanwhile, back at the ranch . . .*
After the prom . . .	*When we got to Archie's place . . .*
Twenty years later . . .	*From my house I could tell . . .*

Transitions of Subject

Consequently . . .

In this manner . . .

On the other hand . . .

In contrast to . . .

Despite all this . . .

One other type of common transition occurs without words. It is the use of spaces, such as skipping lines, starting new chapters, etc.

5. Don't Explain When You Don't Have To

Writers often write long-winded and unnecessary transitions because they are afraid that the short phrase hasn't said enough. In the example below, you can see how the writer slows down the story by trying to *explain* how Sam got to the church when all he needs to do is *acknowledge* that Sam got from his apartment to a church:

> *Sam moved slowly down the stairs of the apartment building. He walked across the street and climbed into his car. He turned the ignition key and put the car in gear. Then he pulled out into Maple Street traffic. When he reached Wilder Avenue, he took a left and drove for three blocks. At Warren Street he waited for a red light that seemed to take forever. Finally he got onto Carver. He could see the Bethany Church up ahead.*

A better transitional sentence appears below:

> *Sam drove to the church.*

Unless something important happened to Sam while driving his car over to the church, don't describe the drive. A transition is simply a bridge and should be used to carry readers as quickly as possible from one place to the next.

6. Use Bridge Words

A bridge word is a word that is used in one paragraph and then repeated in the following transition. It shows you how the writer got from one thought to another, thus supplying you with a smooth bridge between thoughts.

We use bridge words all the time to make conversations smooth. If your friend says, "Let's pick apples Saturday. My brother Larry lives in California," you will feel slightly jarred. You are distracted and will want to ask, "Why are you suddenly talking about your brother?" On the other hand, if your friend says, "Let's pick apples Saturday. My brother Larry and I used to pick apples all the time. He lives in California," the word "apples" provides you with a bridge across your friend's thoughts, and you go along easily.

Similarly, in your writing you can convince the reader of a logical connection between subjects by using good bridge words.

In the March 1982 issue of *Esquire,* Frank Rose wrote an article called "Walking on Water," an update on the California surfing scene. Here's how he used the bridge word "sponsor" to make a logical transition into a discussion of media.

> *Unfortunately, like the good surfing spots, most potenttial sponsors have already been taken.*
> *The scramble for sponsors makes surfers especially media conscious.*

7. Avoid Wordiness

Wordiness has two meanings for the writer. You are wordy when you are redundant, such as when you write, "Last May during the spring," or "little kittens," or "very unique."

Wordiness for the writer also means using long words when there are good short ones available, using uncommon words when familiar ones are handy, using words that look like the work of a Scrabble champion, not a writer.

The following example of wordiness, which I've taken from a letter that appeared in Dr. Adele M. Scheele's "At Work" column, which appears in newspapers all over the country, shows how dull a writer becomes when he or she tries to impress a reader with "intellectual" language.

> *In preparing a list of professional people whose opinion I respect, you are one of the first that comes to mind.*
>
> *It is my objective to more fully utilize my management expertise than has heretofore been the case. . . .*

The letter contains many of the writing mistakes we will discuss in this book, but its greatest fault is wordiness.

The overall tone of the letter is apologetic, meek, uncertain. The writer is babbling. She's trying to find words that are safe because they are vague and they sound very professional to her. By trying to impress the reader with her vocabulary, she is composing a letter that is almost incomprehensible.

Instead of discussing herself, she discusses her "objective," which is "to more fully utilize" her "management expertise." She would have made herself clearer with simple words like "goal," "use," and "skills." Instead of writing about her job, she writes about being confined "to the area of small business and self-employment in the apartment management field," which doesn't tell the reader what she's been doing for a living, only what area she's been doing it in.

Here is a version of that letter that is clear, direct, and simple. It would get a warm reception in any office because the reader doesn't have to struggle to understand it.

> *I've made a list of professional people whose opinion I respect, and your name is at the top of the list.*
>
> *I want to use my management skills more fully. But since I've been running a small apartment management agency for the last six years, I'm a little bit out of touch with the job market. I'd like your guidance and advice so that I can evaluate the market for my skills. . . .*

8. Steal

Be a literary pack rat. Brighten up your story with a metaphor you read in the Sunday paper. Make a point with an anecdote you heard at the barber shop. Let a character tell a joke you heard in a bar. But steal small, not big, and don't steal from just one source. Someone once said that if you steal from one writer, it's called plagiarism, but if you steal from several, it's called research. So steal from everybody, but steal only a sentence or a phrase at a time. If you use much more than that, you must get permission and then give credit. Here are two example of acceptable, honorable ways to steal.

Whenever people ask me what I did for a living before I became a writer, I reply, ''I did all those crummy jobs that would someday look so glamorous on the back of a book jacket.'' It's a cute line, one of many I use often in order to keep myself constantly surrounded by an aura of cleverness. But I didn't invent the line. I read it twenty years ago in a *TV Guide* article by Merle Miller, and I've used it ever since, rarely giving Miller credit for the line.

The previous paragraph shows two examples of acceptable literary theft. The first is Miller's line, which the paragraph is about. The other is the paragraph itself. It's the opening paragraph for an article I wrote in *Writer's Digest* (April 1983) called ''Do Editor's Steal?'' I stole it from myself.

9. Stop Writing When You Get to the End

A novel ends when your hero has solved his problem.

An opinion piece ends when your opinion has been expressed.

An instructional memo ends when the reader has been instructed.

When you have done what you came to do, stop. Do not linger at the door saying good-bye sixteen times.

How do you know when you have finished? Look at the last sentence and ask yourself, "What does the reader lose if I cross it out?" If the answer is "nothing" or "I don't know," then cross it out. Do the same thing with the next to last sentence, and so forth. When you get to the sentence that you must have, read it out loud. Is it a good closing sentence? Does it sound final? Is it pleasant to the ear? Does it leave the reader in the mood you intended? If so, you are done. If not, rewrite it so that it does. Then stop writing.

CHAPTER FIVE

Ten Ways to Develop Style

1. Think About Style

2. Listen to What You Write

3. Mimic Spoken Language

4. Vary Sentence Length

5. Vary Sentence Construction

6. Write Complete Sentences

7. Show, Don't Tell

8. Keep Related Words Together

9. Use Parallel Construction

10. Don't Force a Personal Style

1. Think About Style

In any discussion of writing, the word *style* means the way in which an idea is expressed, not the idea itself. Style is form, not content. A reader usually picks up a story because of content but too often puts it down because of style.

There is no subject that cannot be made fascinating by a well-informed and competent writer. And there is no subject that cannot be quickly turned into a literary sleeping pill by an incompetent writer.

You probably would not buy Ray Bradbury's book *Dandelion Wine* (Doubleday) if while browsing in the bookstore you turned to the version on the left (A). Contrast it with the version on the right (B), Bradbury's actual opening paragraph. You will see that while both paragraphs contain the same information, the version on the right has style, and that makes all the difference.

A	**B**
There wasn't any noise at six A.M., and nobody was up yet. The wind was about the way you'd want it, and everything was pretty much okay. If you got up and took a look out the window, you could tell that summer was beginning.	*It was a quiet morning, the town covered over with darkness and at ease in bed. Summer gathered in the weather, the wind had the proper touch, the breathing of the world was long and warm and slow. You had only to rise, lean from your window, and know that this indeed was the first real time of freedom and living, this was the first morning of summer.*

2. Listen to What You Write

Writing is not a visual art any more than composing music is a visual art.

To write is to create music. The words you write make sounds, and when those sounds are in harmony, the writing will work.

So think of your writing as music. Your story might sound like the *Hungarian Rhapsody No. 2,* or it might sound like "Satisfaction." You decide. But give it unity. It should not sound like a musical battle between the Cleveland Symphony Orchestra and the Rolling Stones.

Read aloud what you write and listen to its music. Listen for dissonance. Listen for the beat. Listen for gaps where the music leaps from sound to sound instead of flowing as it should. Listen for sour notes. Is this word a little sharp, is that one a bit flat? Listen for instruments that don't blend well. Is there an electric guitar shrieking amid the whispers of flutes and violins? Imagine the sound of each word as an object falling onto the eardrum. Does it make a soft landing like the word *ripple,* or does it land hard and dig in like *inexorable*? Does it cut off all sound for an instant, like *brutal,* or does it massage the reader's ear, like *melodious*?

There are no good sounds or bad sounds, just as there are no good notes or bad notes in music. It is the way in which you combine them that can make the writing succeed or fail. It's the music that matters.

3. Mimic Spoken Language

Writing should be conversational. That does not mean that your writing should be an exact duplicate of speech; it should not. Your writing should convey to the reader a *sense* of conversation. It should furnish the immediacy and the warmth of a personal conversation.

Most real conversations, if committed to paper, would dull the senses. Conversations stumble, they stray, they repeat; they are bloated with meaningless words, and they are often cut short by intrusions. But what they have going for them is human contact, the sound of a human voice.

And if you can put that quality into your writing, you will get the reader's attention.

So mimic spoken language in the variety of its music, in the simplicity of its words, in the directness of its expression. But do not forfeit the enormous advantages of the written word. Writing provides time for contemplation. Use it well.

In conversation the perfect word is not always there. In writing we can try out fifteen different words before we are satisfied.

In conversation we spread our thoughts thin. In writing we can compress.

So strive to make your writing sound like a conversation, but don't make it an ordinary conversation. Make it a good one.

4. Vary Sentence Length

This sentence has five words. Here are five more words. Five-word sentences are fine. But several together become monotonous. Listen to what is happening. The writing is getting boring. The sound of it drones. It's like a stuck record. The ear demands some variety. Now listen. I vary the sentence length, and I create music. Music. The writing sings. It has a pleasant rhythm, a lilt, a harmony. I use short sentences. And I use sentences of medium length. And sometimes when I am certain the reader is rested, I will engage him with a sentence of considerable length, a sentence that burns with energy and builds with all the impetus of a crescendo, the roll of the drums, the crash of the cymbals—sounds that say listen to this, it is important.

So write with a combination of short, medium, and long sentences. Create a sound that pleases the reader's ear. Don't just write words. Write music.

5. Vary Sentence Construction

Most sentences have a subject, a predicate, and an object, and early in life we were taught to present them in that order. The dog ate the bone. Dick and Jane jumped into the river. A man walked down the street. Et cetera.

But identical sentence constructions bore readers. Certainly you should strive for clarity and not arrange your sentences in a way that strangles their logic. But you should also keep the primary elements of the sentence dancing so that they will create their own music.

Below are two paragraphs in which all the sentences are constructed the same way. They all begin with the subject, move on to the predicate, and end with an object if there is one. What conclusion about the writer do you draw after reading them?

The Welcome Wagon Lady twinkled her eyes and teeth at Joanna. She was sixty if she was a day. She had ginger hair, red lips, and a sunshine-yellow dress. She said, "You're really going to like it here! It's a

*nice town with nice people! You couldn't have made
a better choice!'' Her brown leather shoulder bag
was enormous. It was old and scuffed. She dealt
Joanna packets of powdered breakfast drink from it.
There was soup mix. There was a toy-size box of non-
pollutant detergent. There was a booklet of discount
slips that were good at twenty-two local shops. There
were two cakes of soap. There was a folder of deodorant pads.*

*Joanna stood in the doorway. Both hands were full.
She said, "Enough, enough. Hold. Halt. Thank you."*

The sentences are all simple constructions—grade school
concoctions. One of the marks of an inexperienced writer
is his or her inability to move beyond these basic sentence
constructions. If Ira Levin's best-selling novel had opened
with those sentences, odds are good it would have been
a *worst*-selling novel. But, it didn't. The actual opening
of Ira Levin's *Stepford Wives* (Random House) follows.
As you read it, take note of the variety of sentence
constructions.

*The Welcome Wagon Lady, sixty if she was a day but
working at youth and vivacity (ginger hair, red lips, a
sunshine-yellow dress), twinkled her eyes and teeth at
Joanna and said, "You're really going to like it here!
It's a nice town with nice people! You couldn't have
made a better choice!'' Her brown leather shoulder bag
was enormous, old and scuffed; from it she dealt Joanna packets of powdered breakfast drink and soup
mix, a toy-size box of non-pollutant detergent, a booklet*

of discount slips good at twenty-two local shops, two cakes of soap, a folder of deodorant pads—

"Enough, enough," Joanna said, standing in the doorway with both hands full. "Hold. Halt. Thank you."

6. Write Complete Sentences

Usually, only a complete sentence expresses a complete thought. A complete sentence has a subject and a predicate. "The cat jumped off the roof" is a complete sentence. "The cat jumped" is also a complete sentence. "The cat," however, is not a complete sentence. You should try to write complete sentences.

However, if your high school English teachers told you that all incomplete sentences were unacceptable, they were wrong. Good writing often contains incomplete sentences. The incomplete sentence is a useful tool. Used wisely it can invigorate the music of your words. Like a chime. Or the beat of a drum.

Here are two examples. The first is from my story, "The Eight Thou." The second is from *Ping* by Gail Levine-Freidus.

"Be damned if I know," Charlie said. He got the cop laughing, then he patted him on the elbow and said, "Hey, look, you got a couple of cigarettes? I could be in this place for a long time. Years maybe."

This is the way Charlie liked to work them. Shoot the breeze. Crack jokes. Butter them up. Be cute. Then hit them for what you really want. He had charmed his way down from Burlington, Vermont, this way, thumbing and lying like a carnival barker all the way into Boston. His real dream was the West Coast. California. But he'd figured a big city like Boston would be the place to stop first and somehow hustle up a couple of hundred bucks for the cross-country trip. Unfortunately, the Boston P.D. hadn't been quite as enchanted by his spiel as some of the people who had given him rides. He hadn't been in town long. Ten days. And this was his third arrest.

When I first arrived, I saw nothing. In time I discovered light. White light. And weightlessness. Then there was motion. For a while I felt as though I were flying. Soaring. Later, I sensed a stillness which held me nearly breathless. Yet, I was unafraid.

Note that the partial sentences are used sparingly. Incomplete sentences do not fare well in large numbers or in groups. They draw their musical strength and often their meaning from the complete sentences that surround them.

So write complete sentences ninety-nine percent of the time. But now and then if a partial sentence sounds right to you, that's what you should write. Period.

7. Show, Don't Tell

Throughout this book I will remind you that shorter is almost always better. This is an exception. It usually takes more words to show than to tell, but you can afford a few extra words for a tool this valuable.

When you show people something, you are trusting them to make up their minds for themselves. Readers like to be trusted. Don't dictate to them what they are supposed to see, or think, or feel. Let them see the person, situation, or thing you are describing, and they will not only like what you have written, they will like *you* for trusting them.

Look at the following letters from camp. Letter A tells; letter B shows. Which letter do you find more revealing: Which letter writer would you rather know—Irma, or Donna?

Letter A

Dear Jan,
My new boyfriend, Arnold, is a terrific athlete. He is also incredibly smart, very sentimental, and sort of strange.

Yours truly,
Irma

Letter B

Dear Jan,
My new boyfriend, Arnold, ran five miles to my cabin in the middle of that lightning storm last week. When he got here, he stood out in the rain and started shouting how he loves me in five different languages.

Yours truly,
Donna

Show, don't tell. Even in business letters and memos.

You want Barbara Resnikoff to get a promotion, but you need the board's approval. Which memo would Barbara Resnikoff prefer to have you send?

Memo A	**Memo B**
Ms. Resnikoff has been loyal, hardworking, and helpful to the company. I think she deserves a promotion.	*Ms. Resnikoff turned down two offers from Westinghouse last year. She worked fourteen-hour weekends, and she saved the Renaldo account even after it was discovered that the rabbit warehouse was empty. She deserves a promotion.*

8. Keep Related Words Together

Words that are part of the same information package are related, and they should be clustered together to avoid confusion. Adjectives should be placed near the nouns they describe so they don't appear to be describing some other noun. Likewise, adverbs should be close to verbs they modify, and dependent clauses should be near the words on which they depend for meaning.

Bad	Better
The boy rode his horse through the winter woods, strong and proud as could be.	The strong, proud boy rode his horse through the winter woods.
Garonovitch saw a small cut on the dog that was on his left front paw.	Garonovitch saw a small cut on the left front paw of the dog.
Nushka's Roumanian pistol misfired when she tried to catch the Chinese bandits, which doesn't happen often.	When Nushka tried to catch the Chinese bandits, her Roumanian pistol misfired, which doesn't happen often.

9. Use Parallel Construction

Though several consecutive sentences constructed the same way can bore the reader, there are times when you should deliberately arrange words and sounds in similar fashion in order to show the reader the similarity of information contained in the sentences. Just as the steady beat of a drum can often enrich a melody, the repetition of a sound can often improve the music of your writing. This is called parallel construction.

Listen to the difference parallel construction makes in the following examples.

Not Parallel	Parallel
I drove to the construction site to see what I could find out from the workers. I talked to the foreman. The electricians and I had a discussion. This was followed by a talk with the carpenters. Also, the plumbers told me what they thought. The same view was held by everybody. The project would have to be started over.	I drove to the construction site to see what I could find out from the workers. I talked to the foreman and electricians. I talked to the carpenters and plumbers. They all said the same thing. The project would have to be started over.
Fish gotta swim, and flying is something that birds must do.	Fish gotta swim, birds gotta fly.
First I came. Then I saw. Conquering came next.	I came. I saw. I conquered.
When one has been seen by you, you've seen them all.	When you've seen one, you've seen them all.

10. Don't Force a Personal Style

Style is not something you can put onto your writing like a new set of clothes. Style *is* your writing. It is inexorably knotted to the content of your words and the nature of you. So do not pour the clay of your thoughts into the hard mold of some personal writing style that you are determined to have. Do not create in your head some witty, erudite, unmistakably exciting persona and try to capture him or her on paper. Also, do not try to write like Erma Bombeck, Hunter S. Thompson, Ernest Hemingway, or anybody else. If you fail you will look foolish, and if you succeed you will succeed only in announcing to the world that you are not very creative. Strive instead to write well and without self-consciousness. Then your style will emerge. It might be as specifically yours as your thumbprint, or it might be as common as sunshine. But at least it will be you.

CHAPTER SIX

Twelve Ways to Give Your Words Power

1. Use Short Words

2. Use Dense Words

3. Use Familiar Words

4. Use Active Verbs

5. Use Strong Verbs

6. Use Specific Nouns

7. Use the Active Voice ... Most of the Time

8. Say Things in a Positive Way ... Most of the Time

9. Be Specific

10. Use Statistics

11. Provide Facts

12. Put Emphatic Words at the End

Twelve Ways to Give
Your Words Power

1. Use Short Words

Short words tend to be more powerful and less pretentious than longer words. *Rape* is a powerful term; *sexual assault* isn't. *Stop* is stronger than *discontinue*.

The fastest way to learn why you should use short words is to read anything by Ernest Hemingway. Hemingway, the Nobel Prize winner who lands on almost everybody's list of great American writers, was a miser when it came to syllables and words. This paragraph, which I picked at random from his *The Sun Also Rises* (Scribner's), contains only two words with more than two syllables.

> *Finally, after a couple more false klaxons, the bus started, and Robert Cohn waved good-by to us, and all the Basques waved good-by to him. As soon as we started out on the road outside of town it was cool. It felt nice riding high up and close under the trees. The bus went quite fast and made a good breeze, and as we went out along the road with the dust powdering the trees and down the hill, we had a fine view, back*

through the trees, of the town rising up from the bluff above the river. The Basque lying against my knees pointed out the view with the neck of a wine-bottle, and winked at us. He nodded his head.

2. Use Dense Words

A dense word is a word that crowds a lot of meaning into a small space. The fewer words you use to express an idea, the more impact that idea will have. When you revise, look for opportunities to cross out several words and insert one. *Once a month* is *monthly; something new* is *novel; people they didn't know* are *strangers;* and something *impossible to imagine* is *inconceivable*.

3. Use Familiar Words

Do you know what a *mandible* is? Your dentist does. He uses that word every day.

So, if you are writing a story just for your dentist, use *mandible*. But if you are writing for everybody else, use the more familiar word, *jaw*.

A word that your reader doesn't recognize has no power. If it confuses the reader and sends him or her scurrying for the dictionary, it has broken the reader's spell.

Familiar words have power. By avoiding very long

words, you avoid most of the words that your reader doesn't know. But you should also replace short words if they are so rare that your reader might not know them.

Even though *delegate* is longer than *depute*, it is better. Don't write *sclerous* if you can·write *hardened*, and if you have written that something is *virescent*, please go back and say that it is *turning green*.

A couple of tips. A word is familiar if it came easily to you but is not part of some specialized knowledge you have, such as a computer term. A word is unfamliar if you never heard of it until you found it in the thesaurus or if you haven't read it at least three times in the past year.

4. Use Active Verbs

Active verbs *do* something. Inactive verbs *are* something. You will gain power over readers if you change verbs of being such as *is, was,* and *will be* to verbs of motion and action.

Bad	Better
A grandfather clock was in one corner, and three books were on top of it.	A grandfather clock towered in one corner, and three books lay on top of it.
As Samson enters the police station, a burly sergeant is behind the desk, and three rookies are around the cor-	As Samson enters the police station, a burly sergeant stands behind the front desk, and three rookies hang

ner talking shop, ignoring
the murder suspect who is
near the open window at the
back of the room.

around the water cooler talking shop, ignoring the murder suspect who edges near
the open window at the back
of the room.

5. Use Strong Verbs

Verbs, words of action, are the primary source of energy in your sentences. They are the executives; they should be in charge. All other parts of speech are valuable assistants, but if your verbs are weak, all the modifiers in the world won't save your story from dullness.

Generally speaking, verbs are weak when they are not specific, not active, or are unnecessarily dependent on adverbs for their meaning.

If you choose strong verbs and choose them wisely, they will work harder for you than any other part of speech. Strong verbs will reduce the number of words in your sentences by eliminating many adverbs. And, more impor-tant, strong verbs will pack your paragraphs with the energy, the excitement, and the sense of motion that read-ers crave.

Sharpen a verb's meaning by being precise. Turn *look* into *stare*, *gaze*, *peer*, *peek*, or *gawk*, Turn *throw* into *toss*, *flip*, or *hurl*.

Inspect adverbs carefully and always be suspicious. What are those little buggers up to? Are they trying to cover up for a lazy verb? Most adverbs are just adjectives with 'ly' tacked on the end, and the majority of them should be shoveled into a truck and hauled off to the junkyard. Did your character really walk nervously, or did he *pace?* Did his wife eat quickly, or did she *wolf* down her supper?

This next passage is from my novel *The Pork Chop War* (Bradbury Press). Version A is loaded with the weak verbs I used in the first draft. Version B is what I published. As you read the passage, pronounce the verbs a little louder than the rest. That's what I do with my students' papers. The sound you will hear is the sound of the engine that is running the story.

Version A	Version B
I stood on the stairs and watched as he got back a bit and forcefully pushed his foot against the door. The door opened up with a screechy metallic sound. Currie went inside. I went quickly down to the doorway to see what would happen. The old lady was on the other side of her kitchen dialing the phone and staring angrily into the air. She pointed the phone receiver at Currie, as if she could shoot him with it.	*I stood on the stairs and watched as he reared back and slammed his foot against the door. The door flew open with the screech of wrenching metal hinges. Currie rushed inside. I ran down to the doorway to see what would happen. The old lady was on the other side of her kitchen dialing the phone and scowling at the air. She aimed the phone receiver at Currie, as if she could shoot him with it.*

6. Use Specific Nouns

Good writing requires the use of strong nouns. A strong noun is one that is precise and densely packed with information.

Be on the lookout for adjectives that are doing work that could be done by the noun. Adjectives do for nouns what adverbs do for verbs; that is, they identify some distinctive feature. They tell you what color the noun is, how it's shaped, what size it came in, or how fast it moved. Adjectives do great work when they are needed. But they are too often brought in when they are not needed. The careless writer drags them in to provide information which would be more interesting if it came directly from the noun. (Who would you prefer to meet, Woody Allen or a guy who knows Woody Allen?)

Before you write a noun that is modified by one or two adjectives, ask yourself if there is a noun that can convey the same information. Instead of writing about a *black dog*, maybe you want to write about a *Doberman*. Do you want to write *large house,* or is *mansion* really to the point? And before you put down *cruel treatment,* ask if you can make a greater impression on the reader with *savagery, barbarity,* or *brutality.*

Read these two sentences:

A man just walked into the room.
A priest just walked into the room.

Were you a little more interested when I told you the man was a priest? That's because he became more specific, and you could see him better. If I had told you that a senator, a garbageman, or a Lithuanian had entered the room, you still would have found him more interesting than a mere man.

Specific nouns have power. In fact, I recently bought a book because of a specific noun. The name of the book is *The Last Goodbye Kiss* by James Crumley (Random House), and I plunked down $2.75 for it after reading Crumley's opening sentence. Read it yourself and see if the same specific noun that forced me to part with my money grabs you.

> *When I finally caught up with Abraham Trahearne, he was drinking beer with an alcoholic bull-dog named Foreball Roberts in a ramshackle joint just outside of Sonoma, California, drinking the heart right out of a fine spring afternoon.*

What specific noun hooked me? *Bull-dog*. If Trahearne had been drinking with an alcoholic *dog,* I might not have bought the book. But the specificity of *bull-dog* brought into focus not only the dog, but also the bar, the beer, and the fine spring afternoon. Why? Because by telling me what kind of dog it was that drank with Trahearne, the author convinced me that he had actually seen the dog. I believed the author's words.

When you take out a general word and put in a specific one, you usually improve your writing. But when you use a specific word, readers assume you are trying to tell them something, so make sure you choose the specific word that delivers the message you want delivered. If your character is driving *a car* down the highway and you change it to *a*

Jaguar, you increase interest, but you also characterize the driver. You build connotations of money and speed. So make sure you choose a car that is consistent with all the other messages you are trying to send the reader.

7. Use the Active Voice ... Most of the Time

When a verb is in the active voice, the subject of the sentence is also the doer of the action.

The sentence "John picked up the bag" is in the active voice because the subject, John, is also the thing or person doing the action of "picking up."

The sentence "The bag was picked up by John" is in the passive voice because the subject of the sentence, bag, is the passive receiver of the action.

Generally the active voice makes for more interesting reading, and it is the active voice that you should cultivate as your normal writing habit. The active voice strikes more directly at the thought you want to express, it is generally shorter, and it holds the reader closer to what you write because it creates a stronger sense that "something is happening."

Listen to how the following passive voice sentences are improved when they are turned into the active voice.

Passive	Active
Dutch drawings and prints are what this book is about.	*This book is about Dutch drawings and prints.*

The light bulb was screwed in crookedly by the electrical engineer.	*The electrical engineer screwed in the light bulb crookedly.*
Blank cassettes and recordings of actual drownings are what's contained in this box.	*This box contains blank cassettes and recordings of actual drownings.*
An even break should never be given to a sucker.	*Never give a sucker an even break.*

Try to use the active voice. But realize that there are times when you will need to use the passive. If the *object* of the action is the important thing, then you will want to emphasize it by mentioning it first. When that's the case, you will use the passive voice.

Let's say, for example, that you want to tell the reader about some strange things that happened to your car. In the active voice it would look like this:

> *Three strong women turned my car upside down on Tuesday. Vandals painted my car yellow and turquoise on Wednesday. The National Aeronautics and Space Administration launched my car into orbit around the moon on Thursday.*

The example shown above is not wrong, but it sounds choppy. To give the story a flow, you would want to use the passive voice, keeping the emphasis on your car:

> *On Tuesday my car was turned upside down by three strong women. On Wednesday my car was painted*

*yellow and turquoise by vandals. On Thursday my car
was launched into orbit around the moon by the National Aeronautics and Space Administration.*

In the passive voice, the car is given emphasis, and the
story about what happened to it has a flow and rhythm
lacking in the first example.

8. Say Things in a Positive Way . . . Most of the Time

Usually what matters is what *did* happen, what *does*
exist, and who *is* involved. So develop the habit of stating
information in a positive manner.

If you want your reader to experience the silence of a
church at night, write "The church was silent." If you
write "There was no noise in the church," the first thing
your reader will hear is the noise that isn't there.

Look at the sentences below and see how much more
effective each one is when written in a positive manner.

Negative	Positive
Renaldo's plan to breed giant rabbits did not succeed.	*Renaldo's plan to breed giant rabbits failed.*
The safe was not closed.	*The safe was open.*
George and Martha were not sober when they got home.	*George and Martha were drunk when they got home.*

This insurance will not cost employees any money.	*This insurance is free to employees.*

Of course, there are times when the negative statement should be used. If it's ten o'clock on a stormy night and your wife was due home at six, you won't call your brother and state the positive: "Jennifer is out." You'll emphasize the negative: "Jennifer is not home yet."

In the sentences below, the negative sentence is stronger than the positive.

Positive	Negative
The President was someplace else during the inauguration.	*The President did not show up for the inauguration.*
Russian athletes were in Russia during the Los Angeles Olympics.	*Russian athletes did not come to the Los Angeles Olympics.*

9. Be Specific

A specific word or phrase is usually better than a general one. The specific word etches a sharper picture and helps your reader to see what you are describing.

Picture a box.

Now picture a black box.

Now picture a black box with shiny silver hinges.

You can see the box more clearly as it becomes more specific.

Of course, there must be a limit to this. I could tell you about a small black box with shiny silver hinges on one end and an inlaid marble top which has a crimson heart painted on it with the most darling cupids dancing around the heart, and so forth. You would see the box, but you would be bored by it and by me.

Try to be specific without being wordy. Don't make a sentence specific by hooking up a freight train of details to it. Make it specific by whittling all the possible word combinations down to those few that say what you want them to say.

General	Specific
She wore two pieces of clothing.	*She wore a bra and panties.*
Recently there was a death in my family.	*On March 5 my father died.*
Various ethnic groups have settled in Worcester.	*Greeks, Italians, and Puerto Ricans have settled in Worcester.*
Some time ago a public official in Montana committed a serious crime.	*Three years ago a Montana senator killed a man.*
My son James is having difficulty with two subjects.	*My son James is flunking math and science.*
Danny Ainge scored well and pulled down several rebounds.	*Danny Ainge scored 35 points and pulled down 18 rebounds.*

10. Use Statistics

A few well-placed statistics will establish your credibility. If they are accurate and comprehensible, they will show the reader that you have done your homework and know what you are talking about. Keep in mind, however, that too many statistics will numb your reader's ability to draw meaning from them. Statistics should be sprinkled like pepper, not smeared like butter.

In the following paragraph from *Everything You Want to Know About Your Husband's Money and Need to Know Before the Divorce* (Crowell, 1980) authors Shelly Aspaklaria and Gerson Geltner use statistics effectively. They establish credibility. But also, by providing the reader with the number of divorces, percentages of women receiving alimony, and some average amounts of alimony, they gave their reader the necessary context in which to view other information in their book.

> *Divorce among couples married more than twenty years has risen annually from 51,000 in 1965 to 72,000 in 1976. These "displaced homemakers" are becoming the nation's "new poor" studies by Congress show. Nationally only one out of seven divorced women (14 percent) receives alimony. Of the millions of divorced women, only 250,000 reported alimony income to the IRS in 1975. The average alimony in the United States in that year was $2,895. The highest average awards were made in Connecticut, about $9,728; Washington, D.C., $5,558; and Massachusetts at $4,122 annually.*

The lowest average alimony awards were granted in North Carolina, $954; Utah, $964; and Maryland, $1,194.

11. Provide Facts

In the following paragraph, the writer has drawn the right conclusions. His statements are factual. But because he is telling the reader his conclusions instead of providing the facts from which the reader can draw his own conclusions, the writing will not have impact.

A lot of banks hand out gifts when you open an account. Since you know that they want your account, it's reasonable to assume that that's the only catch and that the gift is not costing you any money. But sometimes you lose money by taking the gift. In other words, you're getting ripped off.

The above information lacks the facts needed to prove the author's point. Look below at an article Barbara Gilder Quint wrote on the same subject in *Glamour* Magazine's February 1981 issue to see how much more persuasive an author can be with facts.

In New York City one major bank recently advertised a 'free' 19 inch TV set to people who would deposit $3,000 into a 3½ year account that would pay 7% interest.

*But at the same time, other banks were paying 12%
on 2½ year $3,000 accounts—a difference of about
$150 each year in interest on the $3,000, which raises
the question of how 'free' that TV set is.*

12. Put Emphatic Words at the End

Emphatic words are those words you want the reader to
pay special attention to. They contain the information you
are most anxious to communicate. You can acquire that
extra attention for those words by placing them at the end
of the sentence.

If you want to emphasize the fact that redwood trees are
tall, you might write, "Some redwoods are more than 350
feet tall." But if you want to emphasize the fact that one
of the attractions in California is the redwood trees, you
would write, "Also found in California are the 350-foot
redwood trees."

If you want to emphasize the amount of money that
somebody owes you, you write, "By June first please send
me a check for $107.12." If you want to emphasize the
due date, you write, "Please send me a check for $107.12
by June first." And if you want to emphasize who the
check is to go to, write, "On June first the check for
$107.12 should be sent to me."

This is a lesson best learned by ear. Listen to how the
impact of a sentence moves to whatever information hap-
pens to be at the end.

I come to bury Caesar, not to praise him.
I come not to praise Caesar, but to bury him.

Ask what you can do for America, not what America can do for you.
Ask not what America can do for you, ask what you can do for America.

CHAPTER SEVEN

Eleven Ways to Make People Like What You Write

1. Make Yourself Likeable

2. Write About People

3. Show Your Opinion

4. Obey Your Own Rules

5. Use Anecdotes

6. Use Examples

7. Name Your Sources

8. Provide Useful Information

9. Use Quotations

10. Use Quotes

11. Create a Strong Title

Eleven Ways to Make People Like What You Write

1. Make Yourself Likable

In order to write successfully, you don't have to become a great writer. But you do have to make yourself likable. If you are asking people to buy your product, take your advice, mail a check, or worry about the problem you present, you first want them to care about you. When you write well, you share a private moment with the readers. Present yourself to readers as someone they would welcome into their homes. Write clearly and conversationally, and strive always to present in your writing some honest picture of who you are.

Readers will like you if you edit from your work French phrases, obscure literary allusions, and archaic words that are known to only six persons in the world.

Readers will like you if you seem to understand who they are and what their world is like. If you write an article called "Getting Back on the Budget" for *Woman's Day*, and you begin by advising the readers to go out and borrow $100,000, you will reveal your ignorance of the readers' financial status. The readers won't like you.

(And of course the editors at *Woman's Day* won't like you and won't publish your article.)

Readers will like you if you use humor in almost everything you write. Of course, there are times when humor is inappropriate (on a death certificate, for example), but don't hesitate to bring humor into your business correspondence and articles.

Readers will like you if you show that you are human. In a how-to piece, for example, you might write, "This third step is a little hard to master. I ruined six good slides before I got it right. So be smarter than I was; practice on blanks."

2. Write About People

People are why TVs get turned on. People are why books get opened. People are why magazines are purchased. And people are why the well-told tale has been listened to for centuries.

People is the one subject that everybody cares about.

What do other people think? How do they act? What makes them angry, happy, enthusiastic? How will they vote in the next election? How can I get them to fall in love with me, buy my product, support my plan? These are the questions readers ask.

So try to put humanity into everything you write. There are times when you cannot comfortably dress your prose in flesh and blood, but those times are rare. Even a how-to article is about a person named "you."

Don't write about the new bookkeeping system. Write about how the new bookkeeping system will affect people.

If you are writing about the welfare crisis, begin with an anecdote about one family that lives in a car because they cannot pay rent out of their small welfare check.

If you are writing a brochure to attract new members to your church, don't write about the steeple and the organ. Write about the people who come to church suppers, the people who volunteer for committees, the people your readers will meet if they show up for church on Sunday.

3. Show Your Opinion

Few things are duller than a man or woman without an opinion. Your opinion is not always appropriate, but often it is the thing that gives writing its life and color. In fact, it is frequently dishonest to hide your opinion because it will find its way into your writing anyhow by influencing your choice of what material to include and what to ignore.

I often color my stories with my opinion. I think it makes for more interesting writing. But I try to be fair, also. If I put my opinion into the story, I also include opinions of people who don't agree with me.

Below is the lead for an article I wrote about hitchhiking (Worcester Telegram). There's nothing secret about my view of the subject: it's all over the piece. But in that article I also included the views of policemen, parents, kids, and drivers.

*By any rational standard, the idea of hitchhiking—
good Samaritanism in its purest form, people helping
people, etc.—should be a good thing.*

*And yet if you stop any ten people on the street and
ask them about hitchhiking, you will hear the darkest
sort of fumblings. You will hear that hitchhiking is a
bad thing.*

*Hitchhikers are muggers, you will hear, they are
thieves and rapists. And if they are not, then they are
fair and fragile prey for an army of savage cretins that
haunts our highways. Either way, so the story goes,
when hitchhiking takes place, someone is scheduled to
end up in a shallow roadside grave bludgeoned into
oblivion by some highway lunatic.*

*With over 30,000 hitchhiking miles behind me, and
perhaps another 10,000 miles of driving hitchhikers, I
was anything but objective about this. It rankled me to
the core that society had become so concerned about
hitchhiking, and I was convinced that hitchhiking, like
apartment living and late night walks, had been
sensationalized all out of whack by TV and movies.
Every time a hitchhiker shows up on TV, you can bet
somebody is finished.*

By including my opinion in the article, I gave the reader
a basis for discussion, either with other people or in his
own mind. Even if the reader says, "I totally disagree," I
have made him or her think about my subject. I have
accomplished my goal. I don't care if the reader agrees
with my opinion. The important thing is that he or she
respond to it. If you can stir your reader up, then your
writing has achieved some success.

4. Obey Your Own Rules

When you begin to write, you also begin in subtle ways to set down a list of rules, just as you set down the rules at the start of a game. Through your title or first paragraph you communicate to the reader certain guidelines about the subject, the scope, or the tone of the story.

If your title is "Black Mayors in America," you have set a rule that says, "Everything in this story is related to black mayors in America," and you will be violating that rule if you write too heavily about mayors who were not black, black people who were not mayors, or black mayors who were not in America.

If your story begins "Angelica put a spell on Mark three times, and suddenly he found himself craving her body," you have set a rule that says, "Impossible things can happen here." But if you are writing a contemporary love story, and you bring in a witch in chapter nine, you are breaking the rule that says, "This is a true-to-life story," and you will lose your reader.

If you begin your story, "Many people, it seems, weave from their own experience, hopes, fears, and deepest desires a fabric of conviction in UFOs that is so strong it cannot be ripped apart," you have made a rule that says "the tone of this story is serious and respectful of the subject." If you begin, "It seems as if every nut case from Tallahassee to Timbuktu has a scorched circle in his backyard from a flying saucer landing—aliens must be particularly drawn to the mentally ill," you have made a rule that says, "This is going to be a lighthearted look at the subject.'' You must stick with the tone you have established. Readers won't object to any particular tone or rule. They only ask that they be informed and that you don't break the rules you set.

5. Use Anecdotes

An anecdote is a little story or incident that makes a point about your subject. The word comes from the Greek *anekdota* which means *things unpublished,* and ideally your anecdote should be an unpublished incident you discovered in your research. Anecdotes are great reader pleasers. They are written like fiction, often contain dialogue, and reduce a large issue to a comprehensible size by making it personal. Anecdotes crystallize a general idea in a specific way.

Writing a short, colorful anecdote is one of the most compelling ways to begin an article, query letter, or business proposal, and a couple of well-placed anecdotes in your longer stories will break the lock of formality and win your reader's affection as well as his or her attention.

Here is an anecdote which I used to begin a magazine article about psychics (Sunday Morning).

> When Mal Brown of Leominster was a kid, he fell out of an apple tree, got one leg knotted in a branch, tipped upside down, and was yanked to a stop.
> It was a mishap that Brown believes could have killed or seriously injured him, but it didn't. And he

believes it didn't because the Tibetan monk was with him.

"That was the first time I saw the Tibetan monk," says Brown, now the 35-year-old father of three daughters.

Brown says the Tibetan monk, a vision that never speaks, has been with him all his life, helping him out in jams, appearing at moments of jeopardy, offering reassurance that danger will pass.

6. Use Examples

This book is full of examples. I say that something is true, and then I show you an instance of it being true. Because this is a teaching book, many of the examples are long. But examples are usually short in writing. Often they are tacked on to the end of a general statement. They do a lot of work, and they impress readers. Examples are used to back up your statements. They clarify your generalizations and help to prove that you are right. Finally, they show the reader what, exactly, it is that you're talking about.

Below is an example from *Weight Watchers* (April 1982) that shows how I helped prove a point I'd made about foot care.

Most non-specialists don't know much about foot care and that can lead to trouble. For example, Jed Norin's bone spur was originally misdiagnosed as a wart by a general practitioner.

7. Name Your Sources

If your reader works in the downtown area of Austin, Texas, and you write that an earthquake will devastate downtown Austin on February 19, your reader is going to be extremely interested to know where you got your information.

If you mention that you learned of the upcoming earthquake from Ramona Moon Dobbins, a Louisiana swamp witch who saw the whole thing in a vision while she was shuffling her tarot deck, your reader might not be too concerned. But if you mention that your information came from Dr. Winston Ruxbacher, Director of the United States Seismographic Study, your reader might decide that February 19 would be a real good day to skip work and visit an aunt in El Paso.

Your reader's reaction to your information depends on your sources.

Sources are the people you talk to and the literature you read while researching your story. You could mention all your sources in your article or paper, but if you do, you risk losing your reader's attention. Lists of sources can become very boring very quickly.

Decide who or what are your most valuable sources, and name only them. Good sources help build credibility and take on added importance when you are contradicting widely held assumptions, or when a crucial decision depends on your accuracy.

You can note sources informally in the text, or you can include a note on sources at the front or back of your story. Such a note appears below:

Sources

In-depth interviews with Alexander Millis, President, National Wenfronckmonkin Institute, and Randy Freidus, host of the nationally syndicated television show, Your Wenfronckmonkin and You.

Zen and the Art of Wenfronckmonkin *by Jim Bellarosa*
Wenfronckmonkin in the New Age *by Gloria Bunker*
"Wenfronckmonkin: A Male Perspective," article in Macho *magazine, June 1983*

Again, don't include every book you read and every expert you spoke to, just the major sources of information.

You should also include the source of opinions expressed in your story.

If you are expressing your own opinion in a story, don't try to hang it on the vague "There's a growing feeling" or "Widespread opinion is." But neither do you have to precede every sentence with "I think" or "It's my opinion that." If you write, "Sturge Thibedeau is the worst director in Hollywood," that is obviously your opinion, since it is not a measurable fact.

But if you're going to disown the opinion and write something like "Sturge Thibedeau is generally considered to be the worst director in Hollywood," back it up with something like "In a 1981 poll of one hundred top directors, ninety-seven rated Sturge Thibedeau as the worst director in Hollywood or anywhere else." If you can't back the opinion with something, then you have to wonder about where you got the idea in the first place.

I'm not trying to improve your ethics, only your writing. A phrase like *widely regarded* means nothing to the reader unless he or she knows what you mean by *widely regarded*. Does *widely regarded* mean the writer and his brother? Does it mean three bad actors who got canned from Thibedeau's films? Does it mean Sturge Thibedeau's ex-wives? Or does it mean one hundred knowledgeable people in the film industry?

8. Provide Useful Information

Useful information is information that has "service value." That means readers can do something after they read what you have written. They might bake a cake because you gave them a recipe, or they might start getting in shape because you gave them directions for ten exercises. Useful information is often nothing more than a list of places, dates, addresses, or routes. It's not the kind of thing that marks the writer as the next Tom Wolfe, but it is the kind of thing that will make your writing saleable.

9. Use Quotations

"Familiar quotations," wrote Carroll Wilson, in the preface to a book of quotations, "are more than familiar; they are something part of us. These echoes of the past have two marked characteristics—a simple idea, and an accurate rhythmic beat."

Though "quotation" and "quotes" are the same thing, we generally think of quotations as words that are notable enough to have been preserved through time.

Use quotations when you need to enhance an idea with something poetic or reinforce a generalization or an opinion.

Quotations will create the idea that you are not alone in your opinion, that somebody, perhaps even Abraham Lincoln, agrees with you. They will give you credibility by association.

Don't use a lot of quotations, however, or they will look more like crutches to hold you than planks to support you.

How do you come up with good quotations? The most famous source is *Bartlett's Familiar Quotations,* but there are a variety of paperback and hardcover books of quotations. Some are arranged by topic, some by author, some by both. Browse in the bookstore. Also, when you hear a quotation you like, write it down. Here's how you might use a quotation:

"Hold fast to dreams for if dreams die, life is a broken winged bird that cannot fly." The words were written by Langston Hughes, but they have special meaning today for Sturge Thibedeau. Thibedeau, who has long been considered one of Hollywood's worst directors, achieved his lifelong dream yesterday with the release of Treadmill to Oblivion.

10. Use Quotes

Quotes are the words someone said to you when you interviewed her for your story, or short excerpts from some of the reading you did in your research. Quotes in your story will attract readers. The white space surrounding the quotes makes the typed or printed page less intimidating. And, more important, quotes create credibility.

In an article in *Esquire* called "The Height Report," writer Ralph Keyes provided his readers with a lot of nuts-and-bolts information to prove that tall men land better jobs, make more money, and are generally more successful than short men. Here are two examples of how he made those facts stronger and more credible by seasoning his article with quotes from various tall people.

> *John Kenneth Galbraith says he's experienced his tallness as a competitive asset on the job market. At 6' 8.5" he explains, "My height gave me a range of opportunity that I would never have had otherwise, because people always remember the guy whose head stands high above the others when they are trying to think of somebody for a job."*

> *"You send over two people who are equally qualified," the Wall Street recruiter explains, "and they'll pick the taller, better-looking guy every time."*

Quotes must be used judiciously. You can't just hang one up every time you want to cover a hole in your story.

Use a quote when the speaker's words will achieve your goals more effectively than your own words.

Bad	**Better**
There are strong indications that a seedless watermelon will soon be entering the market and that Midwest will be one of the primary distributors.	*Bob Fredola, the nation's leading watermelon expert, told me, "The seedless watermelon is a fact. I've seen it, I've tasted it, and I'm convinced that Midwest will be able to move three million of those suckers in the first year alone."*

The people you interview often say things that are provocative, informative and entertaining. However, they rarely say those things in a concise way. They ramble. They repeat. They reiterate.

If you quote people word for word, most of your quotes will be tedious and half of them will be incomprehensible. Unless national security is at stake, trim your quotes down to the words you need. It is perfectly appropriate to cut the fat from interviews and present to the reader only the meat of what the speaker said. However, cut carefully. A carelessly cut quote can change the meaning of the speaker's words. You must remain true to the spirit of what was said, if not the form.

Bad	**Better**
Governor Cashman leaned back in his chair. "My first	*Governor Cashman leaned back in his chair. "My first*

*wife?'' he said. ''That was
Evelyn, huh? Let me see . . .
Let me . . . No, wait a min-
ute. Let me put it this way.
She was an interesting—
Well, to tell you the truth,
she was a shrew.''*

*wife?'' he said. ''That was
Evelyn, and she was a
shrew.''*

11. Create a Strong Title

A good title will make a reader curious.

A good title is a guide. By telling something about the content of your story, it separates the appropriate readers for your story from those who would have no interest in it.

A good title is short. Don't write, ''Investigative Techniques and Conclusions Concerning the Proposal to Extend Client Services.'' Write, ''Results of the Client Survey.''

A good title hints at the limits of information in the story; that is, it suggests the slant. Don't write, ''How Sports Enriched My Religious Life.'' Write, ''A Christian Looks at Baseball.''

A good title should reveal information, not hide it. Don't write, ''Tips on an Important Purchase.'' Write, ''Six Ways to Save Money Buying a House.''

CHAPTER EIGHT

Ten Ways to Avoid Grammatical Errors

1. Respect the Rules of Grammar

2. Do Not Change Tenses

3. Know How to Use the Possessive Case

4. Make Verbs Agree With Their Subjects

5. Avoid Dangling Modifiers

6. Avoid Shifts in Pronoun Forms

7. Avoid Splitting Infinitives

8. Avoid These Common Mistakes

9. Be Sensitive to Changes in the Language

10. Prefer Good Writing to Good Grammar

1. Respect the Rules of Grammar

To succeed as a writer, you must respect the rules of grammar. If editors or teachers have consistently found grammatical errors in your writing, the flaw in your work is not minor. It is fatal. Good writing and good grammar are not twins, but they are usually found in the same place.

The rules of grammar exist to help you write well, not to sabotage your work, and you cannot write well without them. The rules of grammar organize the language just as the rules of arithmetic organize the world of numbers. Imagine how difficult math would be if three and three equaled six only once in a while or if a tenth was equal to ten percent only when somebody felt like it. Grammatical rules about tense, gender, number, person, and case provide us with a literary currency that we can spend wherever English is spoken or read. Grammar is a system of rules for speaking and writing a given language, and that system was not created just so that English teachers would have something to harass you about. It exists so that we can communicate well, and when you blatantly violate portions of the system, you are chipping away at the stability of the whole.

While you should accept the fact that changes do occur in the language, you should also resist each change every step of the way. Change should not come easily. New words and constructions seeking entry into the language should be met by a mighty army of grammarians saying, "It's wrong," and the rest of us saying, "It just doesn't sound right," so that the trendy, the senseless, and the merely pretty fall dead on the battlefield, and only the truly valuable survive. Change, if I might switch my metaphor, should come gradually and rarely, or the language will fall like a table that has all its legs removed at once instead of replaced one at a time.

2. Do Not Change Tenses

If you begin to write in one tense, you should not switch to another.

Bad	**Better**
We were going over to Tad's house to see his daughter, Riley. When we arrived, Molly says, "The baby just fell asleep, so you can't see her."	*We were going over to Tad's house to see his daughter, Riley. When we arrived, Molly said, "The baby just fell asleep, so you can't see her."*

Each day, John rose from bed and brushed his teeth. Today is different. Today, John doesn't rise from bed at all. The reason? He's dead.

Each day, John rose from bed and brushed his teeth. Today was different. Today, John didn't rise from bed at all. The reason? He was dead.

You have been late for work; your work is of poor quality; and you don't seem to care about this company.

You are late for work; your work is of poor quality; and you don't seem to care about the company.

3. Know How to Use the Possessive Case

Most nouns are made possessive by adding *'s: The dog's paws, a child's toy, the ocean's beauty.* However, if a noun ends in *s* already and is plural, simply add an apostrophe: *The dogs' paws,* A singular noun ending in *s* may be made possessive either way: *The actress's role/The actress' role.*

Wrong	**Right**
My families dogs don't eat table scraps.	*My family's dogs don't eat table scraps.*
The actresses's clothes are over in the corner.	*The actresses' clothes are over in the corner. (More than one actress.)*
All of the girl's hats are on their heads.	*All of the girls' hats are on their heads.*

Deloreses needs are obvious.   *Delores' needs are obvious.*
                                               Or:
                                  Delores's needs are obvious.

When joint possession is being shown, the *'s* usually is added only to the last member of the series: *June and Jane's mother is coming to lunch.* However, if what is possessed is not identical, each noun in the series should have *'s: June's and Jane's teachers are coming to lunch.*

With compound nouns, the *'s* is added to the final word:

My mother-in-law's house is spotless.
The Queen of England's dogs kept barking.

The personal pronoun *it* does not use an apostrophe in its possessive form:

Wrong   **Right**

The dog scratched it's collar.   *The dog scratched its collar.*

The perfume lost it's scent.   *The perfume lost its scent.*

4. Make Verbs Agree With Subjects

Plural subjects require plural verbs; singular subjects require singular verbs. When writing a long or complicated sentence, check to make certain your verb agrees in number with its subject.

Wrong	Right
One of the nicest memories Linda has are those memories of her wedding.	*One of the nicest memories Linda has is the memory of her wedding.* Or: *The nicest memories Linda has are those of her wedding.*
The list of actors who will be in the cast are posted on the bulletin board.	*The list of actors who will be in the cast is posted on the bulletin board.*
The dog, as well as its fleas, are in the car.	*The dog, as well as its fleas, is in the car.* (The number of the subject and verb is not affected by parenthetical phrases introduced by *with, together with, including, as well as, no less than, plus,* etc.)
Will everybody take their pencils out of their desks?	*Will everybody take a pencil out of his or her desk?* (The following nouns are singular: *Each, every, everybody, someone, somebody, no one, anyone,* and *anybody.*)

5. Avoid Dangling Modifiers

A dangling modifier is a word or group of words that appears to modify an inappropriate word in the same sentence. The error occurs most often when passive rather than active verbs are used.

Dangling	Revised
In drawing the picture, his wife was used as the model.	*In drawing the picture, he used his wife as the model.*
To find out who killed him, all the criminals had to be questioned.	*To find out who killed him, I had to question all the criminals.*
Knowing this, and wanting a nice home, a new kitchen had to be installed.	*Knowing this, and wanting a nice home, the Smith family had to install a new kitchen.*

6. Avoid Shifts in Pronoun Forms

Be consistent in your use of a pronoun. Do not switch from singular forms to plural ones.

Inconsistent	Consistent
After one has written a paper, they should take a break.	*After one has written a paper, one should take a break.*

7. Avoid Splitting Infinitives

An infinitive is split when an adverb is placed between the word *to* and a verb.

Bad	Better
She wanted to quickly run the race.	*She wanted to run the race quickly.*
Dave wanted to really make it big as a singer.	*Dave really wanted to make it big as a singer.*
If we were to carefully examine the problem, we could figure out a solution.	*If we were to examine the problem carefully, we could figure out a solution.*

There are times when you will need to split an infinitive in order to make the meaning of your sentence clear. Do so, but do so only when the split is neccessary.

Bad	Better
To go grocery shopping frequently will result in increased spending.	*To frequently go grocery shopping will result in increased spending.*
Atticus Finch wanted to serve justice best.	*Atticus Finch wanted to best serve justice.*

8. Avoid These Common Mistakes

In addition to major grammatical mistakes, there are a good many minor mistakes to be made, and nobody's hands are completely clean. We all have a few grammatical rules that we can never quite nail down despite our "ears" for language. Many people cannot remember the difference between *who* and *whom*. (*Who* is nominative case, and *whom* is objective case, as in "Who is going to the prom with you, and with whom did she go last year?") Many writers use *like* as a conjunction (She walks like she's got a train to catch), even though most grammarians insist it be used only as a preposition (It looks like a luxury car, and it rides like a dream). And almost everybody gets confused about *lay* and *lie*. (And with good reason. *Lay* means to put something down, and *lie* means to recline, but the past tense of *lie* is, would you believe, *lay*.)

Minor mistakes like these might confuse, disturb, or disgust your reader, depending on which mistakes you make, how often you make them, and who the reader is. It's arbitrary. When I wear an editor's hat, I don't mind a writer using *who* instead of *whom*, or occasionally using *like* as a conjunction. On the other hand, I would be inclined to reject the writer who consistently used *like* as a conjunction (even though Shakespeare did it), or who wrote, "I lied down for a nap."

When it comes to minor grammatical mistakes, readers don't all draw lines at the same place. But all readers have a limited number of grammatical mistakes that they will forgive, so you should at least aim for grammatical perfection except when you can improve the writing by breaking a rule of grammar.

Many grammatical errors occur because the writer tries too hard *not* to make a mistake. Instead of trusting his or her ear for language, the writer reacts to some traumatic correction in childhood. Most of us, for example, once said, "Jimmy and me are going to the movies," and had some impolite adult snap at us, "It's 'Jimmy and I are going to the movies.' " Many people were corrected so often that they now change all their *me*'s to *I*'s and write things like "The contract was given to Jimmy and I." (It should be "Jimmy and me." *I* is nominative, *me* is objective.) Or, having been bawled out for saying, "I played bad," when he should have said, "I played badly," the kid turns into an adult who writes things like "I feel badly about your loss," when he means that he feels bad about your loss. The problem is that the writer recalls the specific words involved instead of the pertinent rule, which was not explained.

9. Be Sensitive to Changes in the Language

Even if you know all the rules of grammar, you're covered only for today, not tomorrow. The rules change. Grammar is a living thing; it grows to meet new needs.

An obvious example of this is something called the degenderization of language. The feminist movement has successfully lifted our consciousness about the fact that English pronouns of unspecified gender are always male, a fact that contributes to the idea that males are the regular folk and females are something else. It is good grammar but poor feminism to write, "A doctor should always clean his stethoscope before checking someone's heart."

Several solutions to the problem have been suggested. Among them are *he/she, his/her,* and *s/he.* None has really caught on. What is catching on, however, is "A doctor should always clean their stethoscope," an error in number that is perpetrated by people who would rather offend grammarians than feminists. It's good feminism but bad grammar, and I don't like it. In fact, to be perfectly honest about it, I hate it. But I'm starting to get used to it, and it seems to be earning its way into the language. If it proves to be made of hearty stuff, I will welcome it.

The point is that it's bad grammar today, but it might be good grammar ten years from now. Today's rules have no better shot at immortality than *thee* and *thou* had.

10. Prefer Good Writing to Good Grammar

Keep in mind that good grammar, even perfect grammar, does not guarantee good writing any more than a good referee guarantees a good basketball game.

"It is my objective to utilize my management expertise more fully, than has heretofore been the case" is acceptable grammar but poor writing because it is poor communication. The sentence should read, "I'm looking for a better job." On the other hand, "I ain't got no money" is terrible grammar but could be good writing in some context by communicating *exactly* what the writer wants to communicate.

There are many writing situations in which inferior grammar makes for superior writing. You could use poor grammar to reveal the character of a narrator, as Mac Hyman did in *No Time for Sergeants* (Random House).

> *The thing was, we had gone fishing that day and Pa had wore himself out with it the way he usually did when he went fishing. I mean he went at it pretty hard and called the fish all sorts of names—he lost one pretty nice one and hopped up in the boat and banged the pole down in the water which was about enough to scare a big-sized alligator away, much less a fish, and he spent most of the afternoon after that cussing and ranting at everything that happened.*

You could use poor grammar in an essay or an opinion piece to establish a certain tone: "Marvin Hagler and Ray Leonard go at each other tonight in the Centrum, and it ain't going to be pretty."

You can also use faulty grammar in a story or novel to characterize people, places, and events, or to establish a casual, conversational tone. In this example, poor grammar does both jobs: "Moose asked every guy in the bar if they had seen Helen. Nobody knew nothing. Moose looked like he was going to tear the place apart." There are three grammatical mistakes in those three sentences, but they are all intentional and they are all doing some work.

Whenever you knowingly use poor grammar, you should ask yourself two questions. The first: Is my meaning clear? If the answer is no, rewrite. The second question: What am I getting in return for the poor grammar? If you can't answer that, don't use poor grammar.

So strive most of all for good writing, but make proper grammar your rule and improper grammar your exception. Don't give easy access to every bizarre construction or chunk of senseless jargon that comes whistling down the pike. Never violate a rule of grammar unless you have a good reason, one that improves the writing.

But never choose good grammar over good writing. There is nothing virtuous about good grammar that does not work. Your goal is good writing. Good grammar is only one of the tools you use to achieve it.

CHAPTER NINE

Six Ways to Avoid Punctuation Errors

1. Use Orthodox Punctuation

2. Know When to Use a Comma

3. Know When to Use a Semicolon

4. Know When to Use a Colon

5. Use Exclamation Points Only When Exclaiming and Question Marks Only when Asking Questions

6. Know How to Use Quotation Marks

1. Use Orthodox Punctuation

Writing is not a visual art, so don't use punctuation as decoration. Be creative in your writing, not in your punctuation.

After writing an exclamation, use only one exclamation point. *No!* is every bit as effective as *No!!!*

Avoid using unnecessary quotation marks. Some writers insist on placing quotation marks around slang words: *My "old man" is going to give me some "big bucks."* If you wish to use slang or idioms, do so, but do so without quotation marks.

Avoid using unnecessary dashes and ellipses. Some writers use dashes (— —) and ellipses (. . .) to cover faulty sentence constructions and vague thoughts. Don't.

In the following letter, a young writer uses dashes and elipses the way drunks use whiskey.

Dear Robert,
Well . . . How are you? I'm okay—I guess . . . My
mother came to visit last week—you can imagine how

much fun that was . . . All she did the whole time she was here was search around in my drawers. She was probably looking for drugs . . . or something. Anyhow, you get the picture . . . God!!! So—not much new to report. Take it easy . . . but take it!!!!

Love,
Betsy

2. Know When to Use a Comma

Commas are used to add clarity to a sentence. Consider the sentence below:

She was frightened when he kissed her and fainted.

Without a comma, we don't know who fainted. Perhaps she fainted when he kissed her. On the other hand, perhaps she became frightened because he fainted during the kiss. Only a comma will give this sentence meaning for us:

She was frightened when he kissed her, and fainted.

Ah, *she* fainted.

When deciding whether a sentence you have written needs a comma, read the sentence out loud. Is a pause needed for clarity? Read the sentence without the pause— quickly, if you're still not certain. If the sentence makes perfect sense to you read at breakneck speed, banish that comma. In addition to being wrong, overpunctuation is deadly dull. A good piece of advice: When your ear fails you and you can't decide whether to add that comma, DON'T.

Many otherwise good writers use too many commas. I think one of the reasons is because we were half-asleep in grammar classes as children and never bothered to learn the difference between restrictive and nonrestrictive clauses. Unfortunately, while we must have been sleeping when the terms were explained, we learned just enough to get ourselves in trouble.

Read the sentences below and see which ones require commas:

1. *My friend Pat goes to law school.*
2. *A dance like the limbo requires a broomstick or pole.*
3. *Animals that have fur are fun to pet.*
4. *Do not use a comma unless a pause is needed for clarity.*

The answer? None of the sentences needs a comma. If you read the sentences out loud, your ears should have told you that pauses were not needed. But if you were once one of those children who slept half the time during grammar classes, you might have decided to add commas because the sentences *looked* a lot like sentences that need commas.

Restrictive clauses and words do not require commas. Nonrestrictive words and clauses do. Restrictive elements define and limit a sentence. They must be present for a sentence to retain its intended meaning. Nonrestrictive elements, which are parenthetical, do not.

Look at the following sentences. Notice that in each of

the sentences with nonrestrictive elements, the material contained in commas could be removed without changing the sentence's meaning.

Nonrestrictive	Restrictive
Some dances, like the limbo, require broomsticks or poles.	*A dance like the limbo requires a broomstick or pole.*
One of my friends, Pat, goes to law school.	*My friend Pat goes to law school.*
Snakes, which don't have fur, aren't much fun to pet.	*Animals that have fur are fun to pet.*
Do not use my hairbrush, unless you want to get lice.	*Do not use a comma unless a pause is needed for clarity.*

Here are some other rules to help you with commas:

1. Use a comma following introductory words like *Yes, No,* and *But.* Realize, though, that there are times when such words are not being used as introductions to a sentence.

Wrong	Right
Yes I did take the money.	*Yes, I did take the money.*
My answer is, yes.	*My answer is yes.*
Now, is the time for all good men to come to the aid of their country.	*Now is the time for all good men to come to the aid of their country.*
Now if you take the bus, you'll save money.	*Now, if you take the bus, you'll save money.*

2. Clauses joined by *but* require a comma: *He wanted to eat out, but he didn't have any money*.

3. Use commas *between* members of a series.

Wrong	**Right**
Jim, Jane, and Sue, went to the store.	*Jim, Jane, and Sue went to the store.*

4. Use a comma before a *direct* quotation. (If the direct quotation is long, use a colon rather than a comma.)

Wrong	**Right**
She said "I am a nun and so I can't go out on a date with you."	*She said, "I am a nun and so I can't go out on a date with you."*
She said that, "She was a nun and so she couldn't go out with me."	*She said that she was a nun and so she couldn't go out with me.*

5. Following a person's name, set off by commas information indicating residence, position, or title.

Wrong	**Right**
Mr. and Ms. Smith-Johnson of Portland, Oregon were at the ball.	*Mr. and Ms. Smith-Johnson, of Portland, Oregon, were at the ball.*

6. Use a comma to separate elements of a sentence that might be misread.

When happy, men and women tend to smile.

If I make a will, will I ever be able to change it?

In addition to the rules above, there are many others. I've tried to review the ones that give writers the most trouble. If you have other questions about commas, I suggest reading *Words Into Type* (Prentice-Hall).

3. Know When to Use a Semicolon

The semicolon signals a distinct pause in a sentence. Use it when a comma would not give your sentence sufficient pause.

1. Use a semicolon to separate closely related independent clauses that are not joined by a conjunction.

Nushka looked at the clock; Nanette looked at the floor.

Not all sailors love the sea; not all garbage men love garbage.

2. Use a semicolon to separate word series that contain commas.

They bought soda, potato chips, ice cream, and candy; several games and toys; and three record albums.

4. Know When to Use a Colon

Colons are used to introduce lists, formal quotations, and examples:

> *Please bring the following items: cups, sugar packets, spoons, nondairy creamers, napkins, coffee, and coffeepots. We will bring everything else required to make the coffee.*

> *In Act I of* Falling Bodies, *Bernice speaks of a white cross: "We used to lie in our beds at night and watch this sign on top the life insurance building. . . ."*

> *JoDean wants to become a nun for the wrong reasons. For example: She speaks endlessly about how upset her ex-boyfriend will be when she enters the convent; she speaks endlessly about how she will get to wear a habit; and she speaks endlessly about how nice it will be to have her own bedroom.*

5. Use Exclamation Points Only When Exclaiming and Question Marks Only When Asking Questions

Most of us presume we know when to use question marks and exclamation points. But both punctuation marks have given many good writers trouble.

Exclamation points should be used only after commands

or statements of strong feeling. Only teenagers are justified in believing that each and every statement one utters is an exclamation. The rest of us should know better. Trust your sentences to reveal emotions. Don't rely on punctuation to show how much feeling you bring to your writing.

Bad	**Better**
It's easy to cut men's hair! Just get yourself a man, a pair of scissors, and a bowl!	*It's easy to cut men's hair. Just get yourself a man, a pair of scissors, and a bowl.*
Gertrude said, "Honestly! I'm not a moron!"	*Gertrude said, "Honestly! I'm not a moron."*

There are two instances when writers misuse question marks. First, a question mark should be used only to ask a direct question, not to express wonderment. Second, a question mark is not used to ask an indirect question.

Wrong	**Right**
I wonder why she isn't here? He asked how old Judy was?	*I wonder why she isn't here. He asked how old Judy was.*

6. Know How to Use Quotation Marks

All words taken directly from another's speech or writing must be set off in quotation marks.

Wrong	Right
He said, Sometime I will, and then he walked away.	*He said, "Sometime I will," and then he walked away.*
It was Shakespeare who wrote, To be or not to be.	*It was Shakespeare who wrote, "To be or not to be."*

Do not use quotation marks around words that are not directly taken from speech or writing.

Wrong	Right
He said that "Sometime he would," and then he walked away.	*He said that sometime he would, and then he walked away.*
Hamlet wanted both "to be and not to be," and so he couldn't bring himself to commit suicide.	*Hamlet wanted both to be and not to be, and so he couldn't bring himself to commit suicide.*
She told them to "Get up in the morning."	*She told them to get up in the morning.*
	Or:
	She told them, "Get up in the morning."

If a quote is contained within another quote, use single quotation marks around the inner quote.

Wrong	Right
"Do you know what Bernice said?" JoDean asked. "She said, "I'll be dead in the morning." "	*"Do you know what Bernice said?" JoDean asked. "She said, 'I'll be dead in the morning.' "*

Use quotation marks around a word or phrase you intend to explain or define.

Wrong	**Right**
Nervous breakdown refers to a complete collapse and not to a slight feeling of depression.	*"Nervous breakdown" refers to a complete collapse and not to a slight feeling of depression.*
What is meant by nuclear meltdown?	*What is meant by "nuclear meltdown"?*
I use the word hopeful only when I mean full of hope.	*I use the word "hopeful" only when I mean "full of hope."*

Or:

I use the word <u>hopeful</u> only when I mean "full of hope."

Titles of articles in magazines, poems, songs, paintings, and sermons are set off in quotation marks:

Wrong	**Right**
My favorite Beatles song is ELEANOR RIGBY.	*My favorite Beatles song is "Eleanor Rigby."*
Did you read <u>One Million Ways to Lose Weight</u> in "Glamour" or in some other magazine?	*Did you read "One Million Ways to Lose Weight" in <u>Glamour</u> or in some other magazine?*

The words *Yes* and *No* are put in quotation marks only when they are directly quoted:

Wrong	Right
She could not say "no" to her mother.	*She could not say no to her mother.*
Tell her "No."	*Tell her no.*
She looked me in the eye and whispered no.	*She looked me in the eye and whispered, "No."*

CHAPTER TEN

Twelve Ways to Avoid Making Your Reader Hate You

1. Avoid Jargon

2. Avoid Clichés

3. Avoid Parentheses

4. Avoid Footnotes

5. Don't Use Transitions to Conceal Information

6. Don't Acknowledge When You Should Explain

7. Don't Hide Behind Your Words

8. Don't Intrude

9. Don't Play Word Games.

10. Don't Play the Tom Wolfe Game

11. Don't Play the Mystery Game

12. Don't Cheat

1. Avoid Jargon

Jargon is nonsensical language, unintelligible words, or phrases that somehow get a foothold in the language and are repeated so often that we forget they don't mean anything. Shallow phrases such as *in terms of, in point of fact,* and *interface situation,* are jargon.

We're all guilty. I use jargon. You use jargon. From time to time every person utters something that is without meaning or doesn't mean what he or she wants it to mean. In spoken language this is forgivable; after all, when we speak, we're all working in the first draft. But writers should certainly be able to keep jargon under control.

Because I can't possibly cover thoroughly the subject of jargon here, I recommend two books: *Strictly Speaking* by Edwin Newman (Bobbs-Merrill), and *On Language* by William Safire (Times Books).

Here's a tip: If you can make a man sound like an idiot simply by quoting him, he's probably using jargon.

Bad	Better
I advise you to remain unambulatory for the next six weeks.	*Don't walk for six weeks.*
We believe these improvements will lead to enhanced learning environments.	*We believe these improvements will lead to better classrooms.*
The forthcoming regulations have been instituted due to the increasing incidence of postschool vandalism.	*There's been a lot of vandalism after school, so I've made some new rules.*

2. Avoid Clichés

Clichés are a dime a dozen. If you've seen one, you've seen them all. They've been used once too often. They've outlived their usefulness. Their familiarity breeds contempt. They make the writer look as dumb as a doornail, and they cause the reader to sleep like a log. So be sly as a fox. Avoid clichés like the plague. If you start to use one, drop it like a hot potato. Instead, be smart as a whip. Write something that is fresh as a daisy, cute as a button, and sharp as a tack. Better safe than sorry.

3. Avoid Parentheses

Parentheses are used to enclose material that would otherwise be an annoying interruption. If you are using parentheses more than three times in a ten-page story, you are either interrupting the reader too much, or you are using parentheses unnecessarily. The writer usually turns to parentheses out of laziness, not out of need, and there is usually an unobtrusive way to include the information without parentheses.

Mark Twain wrote, "A parenthesis is evidence that the man who uses it does not know how to write English or is too indolent to take the trouble to do it; . . . a man who will wantonly use a parenthesis will steal. For these reasons I am unfriendly to the parenthesis. When a man puts one into my mouth, his life is no longer safe."

Twain, as you can see, didn't much care for the parenthesis.

I wouldn't say you should never use parentheses, but I think you should use them rarely.

Bad	Better
Parentheses are used to enclose material which would otherwise be an annoying interruption. (A humorous observation, for example.)	*Parentheses are used to enclose material which would otherwise be an annoying interruption, such as a humorous observation.*

4. Avoid Footnotes

Footnotes are a requirement for research papers and are sometimes necessary for other kinds of writing. They are used to acknowledge sources, and sometimes they provide the reader with supplementary material that is valuable to the reader but not compatible with the overall tone of the story.

Use them if you must for those purposes. But please don't use footnotes as a junkyard for all the words you cut from the text but couldn't bear to part with. Footnotes are distracting, ugly, and they frequently work against you because the reader can't remember what he knows from the text and what he knows from the footnotes.

The last word on this matter belongs to John Barrymore. He said, "A footnote in a book is like a knock on the door downstairs while you are on your honeymoon."

5. Don't Use Transitions to Conceal Information

As a writer, you have entered a covenant with the reader. The whole writing reading process depends on the writer and reader having faith that the other will not violate the terms of the covenant. If the covenant were written out, it would contain a clause concerning transitions that would look like this:

Reader agrees that a transition such as "Sam drove to the church" can encompass all the routine acts of starting a car, taking left turns, etc.

In turn Writer agrees not to use such transitions to deprive reader of information which belongs to Reader.

In other words, you shouldn't use the transition "Sam drove to the church" if later in your story you are going to mention that Sam had a horrible accident and killed a carload of lawyers while driving to the church.

Don't cheat readers on the grounds that you wish to surprise them later in the story. Readers know the difference between being cheated and being surprised.

6. Don't Acknowledge When You Should Explain

Many writers try to force transitions to do work that should have been done by the writer elsewhere in the story or article.

In the 1930's, adventure serials with cliff-hanger endings were popular in the London monthlies. At the end of one installment, the writer had his hero, Ben, trapped at the bottom of a dark and slippery twenty-foot pit with no tools, no ladder, and nobody around to hear his cries. For a month people all over London discussed Ben's plight. How would good old Ben get out of this mess? Unfortunately, the writer of the serial was wondering the same thing, and by the time his deadline arrived he had not come up with a clever solution. So he began his episode with, "After Ben got out of the pit, he proceeded to walk toward the city," a transition which put his readers into a lynching mood and did serious damage to the writer's career.

"After Ben got out of the pit" would be a perfectly decent transition if climbing out of a twenty-foot pit were as routine an activity as driving to a church. The reader will accept your acknowledgment of changes in time or place only if those changes could have been accomplished in normal, routine ways, or in unusual ways that you have made believable earlier in your story. If you tell us on page 1 that Superman can fly, we will have no trouble later on accepting the transition "On Tuesday Superman flew to Clinton, Massachusetts."

When you find yourself having difficulty moving from one section of an article to the next, the problem might be due to the fact that you are leaving out information. Rather than trying to force an awkward transition, take another look at what you have written and ask yourself what you need to explain in order to move on to your next section.

7. Don't Hide Behind Your Words

You should be willing to put yourself into what you write. That doesn't mean you should write everything in the first person, or that you should meticulously insert your feelings and observations into every memo. What it does mean is you should not be afraid to climb onto the page when your presence will strengthen what you have written.

Let's say there's a disastrous hotel fire in Providence, Rhode Island, and you were staying in the hotel at the time. It would be unthinkable to leave yourself out of the story. You, after all, are an eyewitness. You felt the heat, you saw the people leap from windows, you heard the lower floors cave in beneath you. Your experience, your feelings at the time, can bring the reader right into an article like nothing else:

> *At noon on August 3, I was in Room 1104 of the Westcott Hotel, just five floors above a flame that would eventually consume the entire hotel and take 118 lives.*

But if you were in Amarillo, Texas at the time of the Providence fire and were assigned three months later to write a story about it, your experience at the time is of no relevance to your article, and so it would be foolish to write the following:

> *At the time of the Providence hotel fire I was in Amarillo, Texas swilling down piña coladas with William F. Buckley.*

If you decide it is best to put yourself into a story, do so with confidence and enthusiasm. Don't creep shyly in with some absurd device like "This reporter witnessed the events," or the pretentious "We" when you mean "I."

In other words, don't be coy about involving yourself in what you write.

8. Don't Intrude

If you are going to put yourself into an article, memo, or story, do it early.

It's okay to begin your profile, "I met Jane Fonda at the Top of the Pru in Boston. She was staring out at the Boston skyline. She was startled when I touched her."

On the other hand, you are intruding if you have written forty-three paragraphs about Jane Fonda, all without mentioning yourself, and suddenly let drop; "She turned to me then, the weariness showing in her face, and I thought for a moment that she would place her head on my shoulder."

Don't make the reader ask the question: Where the hell did *he* come from?

Here are some other types of intrusions you must avoid:

1. Typographical and spelling errors, as well as blatant grammatical errors, will break the reader's spell. They will remind him that he is reading:

   Now is the time for all goodmen to come to the aid of their country.

2. Obscure words, difficult words, and words that don't come within a mile of the meaning you are assigning to them will also break the reader's spell.

   Van was the cotyledon of the family, and Donna, the youngest, was of course the coup de grâce.

3. Using the same word in unrelated ways two or three

times in a short space will also intrude on the reader's trance.

The night was still and quiet. From our position on the hillside we could see that the still was still there.

9. Don't Play Word Games

Puns, double entendres, rhymes, inside jokes, and various other literary parlor tricks are amusing, and they can be good writing in a story that is intentionally whimsical. But generally you should stay away from them in your writing. They might make you look clever, but they will diminish the success of the writing. The reader sees too much of form and loses track of content. Quite often the reader will chuckle at your cleverness but will cease to take your story seriously.

It is often when searching for the perfect title that a writer falls prey to word games. Don't call an article about a coyote that has escaped from the zoo ''Don Coyote.'' Please.

10. Don't Play the Tom Wolfe Game

If you have read any of Tom Wolfe's early books, you know that Wolfe employed a lot of visual GIMMICKS like

ZOWeeee!!!!!, lively little passages full of CAPITAL LETTERS, and unUSual Punk Chew A Shun. . . .!!!?

I call that the Tom Wolfe game, and it was fine for Wolfe. It was fun. It worked. It became part of his writing personality. It's his.

But ninety-nine percent of the time this sort of thing fails. It draws attention to the gimmick and away from the content. It reminds readers that they are reading, and it occasionally brands the writer a moron.

Certainly the appearance of your story is not irrelevant. Clean paper, bold print, white space—all of these things affect the success of the story. But writing is not primarily a visual art. It is more like music than oil painting, and the extent to which it must depend on the shape, size, and color of those squiggly little lines is the extent to which it is not writing, but is something else.

If you cannot state a good reason for doing SOMEthing LYKE Thhhhiiiissss!!!, don't do it.

11. Don't Play the Mystery Game

You are playing the mystery game when you withhold some vital piece of information because you think the reader will hang in there until the end just to find out what it is. More likely the reader will be distracted by the unanswered question and will not pay close attention to what you write.

In *On Becoming A Novelist* (Harper & Row), John Gardner put it this way: "One of the most common mistakes among young writers is the idea that a story gets its power from withheld information—that is, from the writer setting the reader up and then bushwhacking him. Ungenerous fiction is first and foremost fiction in which the writer is unwilling to take the reader as an equal partner.''

Every writing teacher has read hundreds of unpublished stories that begin with something like ''The package arrived at two A.M. Sammy opened it in a frenzy; he stared at its contents and smiled.'' The story goes on and on, and we hear a lot about ''it'' or ''the contents of the package.'' If we stick around long enough, we discover in the last paragraph that the package contained an adorable beagle puppy.

Another common version of the mystery game occurs in the first-person story. We don't learn until the end that the speaker is not a person at all but a 1957 nickel or an oak tree. This is silly stuff. Gardner describes it as the writer jumping out at the last minute and yelling, ''Surprise!'' It's also an extremely efficient way to drive away readers.

Similarly, when writing a paper for a school assignment, bring the statement you wish to prove into the paper's beginning, and then prove your statement. Don't wait until you are almost finished with your paper to mention what it is you are writing about.

12. Don't Cheat

Readers expect writers to be honest. Don't let them down. Even when writing fictional stories, don't mislead readers or hide facts from them. Especially, don't lie.

Adhere to the guidelines below, and readers will reward your honesty by believing in your words.

Don't	**Do**
Don't obscure the quotes you use. If Mr. Green said, "I, uh, uh, occasionally have a drink," don't edit the quote so that it reads, "I . . . drink." The meaning of the two quotes is different.	*Do show compassion for those you quote. If Mr. Green said, "I, uh, uh, occasionally have a drink," there is no reason to include Mr. Green's stammers in your quote (unless you are trying to prove that Mr. Green is not an effective speaker). Your quote should read, "I occasionally have a drink."*
Don't present another's idea as your own. If you are writing about the water imagery in Shakespeare's comedies and you read a book by Rosemary Gilvary in which there is a list of all the water imagery in Shakespeare's comedies, you must give Ms. Gilvary credit if you make use of the list.	*Do give credit where credit is due.*
Don't ignore facts. If you are writing a paper in which you want to prove that smoking marijuana will lead to	*Do show how the other side feels, and do present facts that the other side would use to refute you. Such facts can be used to your advantage.*

lower grades in school, you should not ignore facts that run contrary to your argument. If you discover that several outstanding scholars have smoked marijuana, you should reveal that fact and find a way to incorporate it into your argument, perhaps by saying that these scholars would have performed even better had they not smoked marijuana.

Don't pretend to have proved something you haven't proved. If you write a memo in which you insist that employees must stop taking fifteen-minute coffee breaks because company policy forbids them, do not conclude your memo by writing, "Employees who take fifteen-minute coffee breaks make more work for those of us who limit ourselves to ten-minute coffee breaks." If you wanted to make that statement, you should have written a memo in which you proved it.

Do consider what it is you want to prove, and then spend your time proving it.

Don't lie. Occasionally, a writer will be tempted to write something that isn't true. Are all boxing fans bloodthirsty? If not, don't write that they are. Be careful to point out what is your opinion as opposed to what is a fact.

Do introduce opinions as opinions, and not as facts.

CHAPTER ELEVEN

Seven Ways to Edit Yourself

1. Read Your Work Out Loud

2. Cut Unnecessary Words

3. Think About What You Have Written

4. Ask Yourself These Questions

5. Follow These Rules of Form for Titles

6. Prepare a Perfect Manuscript

7. Use Common Sense

1. Read Your Work Out Loud

Before you turn in anything you have written—whether to a teacher or an editor—read aloud every word.

Often when you write and rewrite and constantly re-arrange information, your ear for the sound of the writing becomes corrupted. Reading out loud will return to you the true sound of your story. You will hear the sour note of the word that's "just not right," and the drastic changes in tone will cry out to you for editing. You'll notice that you are breathless at the end of one long sentence, and you will know that you must break it up into two or three. Listen for the music, variety, and emphasis of your sentences. You will discover that some of them are confusing and need a word added or removed for clarity's sake. And you will see that a sentence like "Who knew that Lou cued Sue, too?" might not *look* funny, but it sure makes a funny and distracting noise in the reader's head.

2. Cut Unnecessary Words

Let's pretend your mechanic called you up and said, "Mr. Duckworth (assuming your name is Mr. Duckworth), your car is ready. I've put in a new carburetor, an alternator, two hoses, a couple of clamps, and three unnecessary parts."

What would you think of such a phone call?

Hmnn. You might think it's time to get a new mechanic.

You don't want unnecessary parts in your car. They do no good, and they slow you down.

So you certainly don't want unnecessary words in your writing. They do no good, and they slow you *and* your reader down.

Every word you write should be doing some work in the sentence. It should earn its keep by providing some portion of the total information you are trying to communicate. A word is unnecessary if it's doing no work, if it's doing work that doesn't have to be done, or if it's doing work that's being done by another word or phrase nearby.

Read what you have written and cross out every word that is not contributing information. Sometimes you will cross out two words and replace them with one. Sometimes you will cross out ten words and replace them with five. But most of the words you cross out will require no replacement.

Bad	**Better**
The annual ball is held once a year in Quincy.	*The annual ball is held in Quincy.*

It is my opinion that rock and roll will live forever.	*I think rock and roll will live forever.*
In the event of rain, the picnic will be held on Monday.	*If it rains, the picnic will be held Monday.*
I would like to say that she was wrong.	*She was wrong.*
Tom proceeded to thread the needle.	*Tom threaded the needle.*
At that point in time I was still wearing hats.	*Then, I wore hats.*
The suspect was driving a 1981 Chevrolet, blue in color.	*The suspect was driving a blue 1981 Chevrolet.*
It has come to my attention that employees are spending too much time at the water cooler.	*Employees are spending too much time at the water cooler.*

3. Think About What You Have Written

It's very easy when you are locked in the passionate embrace of the writing muse to write something that sounds really dumb. The writer routinely includes the banal, the inaccurate, and the just plain stupid in early drafts simply by forgetting that what one meant to say is not always what got written down.

But when the passion cools a bit and the writer spreads his or her papers out on the table, curious phrases will suddenly show themselves: Did she mean to write, "There was literally an ocean of people . . ."? Of course not. But she did. Did he intend to write, "He could care less . . ."? No. He meant to write, "He couldn't care less."

You will make mistakes in your early drafts. That's okay. But before you type a final draft, let at least a day pass, and then think carefully about what you wrote before turning to your typewriter. You may find that what you thought was brilliant prose on Tuesday borders on the moronic by Friday. On the other hand, you may discover that what seemed trivial when you wrote it is, in fact, profound.

4. Ask Yourself These Questions

Before typing a final draft, ask these questions:

1. Is it clear from the beginning what the paper is about?
2. Does each paragraph advance the subject?
3. Do the important ideas stand out clearly?
4. Are more details, examples, or anecdotes needed?
5. Is the information sufficiently clear?
6. Are there sweeping statements that need to be supported?
7. Do any technical terms need explanation?
8. Is there needless repetition?
9. Is the tone consistent?
10. Are any of the sentences too involved to follow with ease?

11. Are any of the words vague?
12. Are there grammatical errors?
13. Are there punctuation errors?

5. Follow These Rules of Form for Titles

Before typing a final manuscript, review these rules for titles:

1. The title of a book-length manuscript should be typed on a separate page, together with the author's name. Set the title at the very center of the page. The author's name goes below the title.
2. Titles of short manuscripts should be centered at the top of the first page of your paper or story.
3. Capitalize titles in the following manner:
   > *The Needs of Some Chickens*
   > *The Ballerina: A Study of America's Most*
   >   *Beloved Dancers*
   > *Of Mice and Men*

   Prepositions that have fewer than four letters should not be capitalized unless they are the first word of the title. Similarly, only capitalize definite and indefinite articles if they are the first word of the title.
4. Use italics (underlining) for titles of books, magazines, movies, and plays.
5. Use quotation marks around the titles of articles, short stories, poems, songs, and other short pieces of writing.

6. Prepare a Perfect Manuscript

If you are proud of the words you have written, you will want to present them in the best possible manner.

Use 8½″ × 11″ white bond paper of good quality. Don't use onion skin or erasable paper—the print will smudge.

Use a clean, black typewriter ribbon. If the keys of your typewriter are dirty, clean them with a brush.

Leave wide margins—at least an inch on all sides of the paper.

Indent five spaces for a new paragraph.

Double-space between lines.

After typing your paper or story, look for typographical errors. Correct small errors with a pencil. Large errors, such as a missing sentence, may force you to retype a page. Use your judgment.

7. Use Common Sense

I write often about writing, and that can be terrifying. Sometimes I feel as if I'm standing in front of a firing squad and The Captain will give the order to shoot as soon as I have violated my own advice. Have I used too many words to tell you not to use too many words? Is my voice too passive when I tell you to use the active voice? Is my grammar faulty when I tell you to bone up on your grammar?

It is not hard to imagine a legion of mean-spirited

readers out there scanning my every word with a magnifying glass, all of them poised to leap on the first sign of contradiction. Off to their typewriters they will run, and soon my mailbox will be bent from within by a bulging bundle of letters, all of which begin, "Dear Mr. Provost, on page such and such you said so and so, but just thirty-two pages later you said so and so and such and such. Are you a moron?"

No, I'm not. Honestly. I am—dare I say it—an artist. And that is my escape hatch. Writing is art, not science, and when I finish a piece of writing, I do not review every single one of my tips. I ask, have I communicated well? Have I pleased my readers, have I given them something that is a joy to read? Have I entertained them, informed them, persuaded them, and made my thoughts clear to them? Have I given them what they wanted?

And these are the questions you must ask about all that you write. If the answers are yes, you have succeeded. If the answers are no, you have failed. Writing well is what counts.

The tips in this book encompass much of the accumulated knowledge about what writing techniques work best, which patterns of language most successfully reach and hold readers. But like all tips they should be considered carefully before being acted on.

So don't use the active voice "because it's the right way." Don't write with strong nouns and verbs "because you're supposed to." And don't maintain consistently good grammar "because only stupid people don't." Tips, not laws. Think about these tips. Apply them generally. They will guide you to successful writing.

And do something else. Accept the fact that there is

good writing and bad writing. There is writing that runs, and there is writing that plods. There is writing that wakes up readers and writing that puts them to sleep. So turn to this book from time to time. Stretch your vocabulary. And, most important, develop your ear for the sound of written language. When you have done these, you will have the knowledge and the wisdom to apply the best tip of all: Use your own common sense.